ACKNOWLEDGEMENTS

I would like to gratefully acknowledge the wonderful dream information shared with me by so many people and in particular I would like to thank Chris, Christopher, Matt, Clare, Colette, Mary, Attracta, Jim, James, Eileen, Maureen, Lisa and Roy.

INTRODUCTION

'Give me a fish, I eat for a day.
Teach me to fish, I eat for a lifetime.'

A self-help guide to analysing your dreams.

Have you ever had a sense that despite what other people have told you, even close family members, that there is more to life than what they are telling you, and that you can have a life far greater than the one that they have planned for you?

Opportunities in life are not taken by the faint hearted, instead they are seized by those people who have a sense of their own destiny, and have the courage of their convictions to step outside the square that has been prescribed for them by their family and friends.

It is this sense of something greater, that encourages these few hardy souls to have an open minded approach to life and to ask questions, believe no one and check every thing out.

By trusting their own intuition, they search for answers rather than allowing themselves to be manipulated into situations by their ego that they may regret later.

Destiny is something that we either do or do not believe in, that sense of fate, for good or evil that a higher power has laid out for us, regardless of our free will and choice.

And then again, sometimes life is really only a matter of faith, a faith in oneself and a faith in ones ability to shine, to stand out from the crowd or to make a difference in life and at the end of life be able to say, "I have lived!"

The opportunity to make this happen depends on the determination of the individual to make it happen.

Opportunities will present themselves when the ground work has been laid, and we have the courage to take that leap of faith.

One talented young Irish comedian that I know, spent years and money getting professional training to hone his skills, but was unsuccessful in finding opportunities in his chosen career.

Then, while on a holiday visiting friends, a gesture of good will by that friend, provided him with an unexpected opportunity to show-case his talents, resulting in being talent spotted by an agent, and he has not looked back since, simply going from strength to strength.

The ground work had already been done, and so when the opportunity presented itself, the comedian was ready to take it.

Call it good luck, or call it fate, or just good timing, but whatever we choose to call it, the person themselves is responsible for their success, as they had a belief in their talents and a dream of what they wanted to do, and so put the time and effort into being ready for when the opportunity was available.

The old adage; "Fail to prepare, prepare to fail" applies to everyone.

How many of us also have a dream, but it only remains a dream, as we do not make the necessary changes to our lifestyle that the dream requires, we do not prepare a solid foundation for our dream to be built on?

We neglect the urgings of the soul in our dreams that is pushing us to change, to grow to be successful, to stop sabotaging ourselves, we dismiss it all as just a dream, because it is just too much of an effort, to make the necessary changes to be successful and even if we did become successful, would we be happy we ask ourselves and so we justify our inertia and do nothing.

By paying attention to our dreams we are able to get information from many sources, and depending on how spiritually evolved we are, and how honourable our intentions, as well as depending on how healthy our mental outlook is, we will find ourselves privy to information, that will provide the dreamer with a healthy, happy, and profitable life.

Even those individuals who are more concerned about the day to day business of their lives, need not feel that they miss out on opportunities. They can rest assured that those family members, who are already in spirit, will continually put opportunities the way of the living, and encourage that, 'inner knowing' feeling, to enhance their lives in some way.

However, by consciously becoming aware of the information being sent to us in our dreams, we are more confidently able to go in the direction of our dreams. And we are able to do this despite perhaps, a lack of support from significant others, or from friends who may pour cold water on our aspirations, because they themselves, may lack the necessary confidence, to go in the direction prompted by their own dreams or inner voice.

Many times I see clients who bemoan the fact, that no matter how hard they try, they can never understand the meaning of their dreams, or else they cannot remember their dreams, and I explain that there is a quick way to access dreams that will provide them with the necessary courage, or confidence to make an urgent decision.

It is a wise person however, who takes the time to write down their dreams on a regular basis, as three weeks before, or three weeks after the anniversary of the death of a loved one, an opportunity is sent to each family member from the deceased relative, to enhance their lives in some way.

The Celtic belief, in the cauldron of life, that provides nourishment for the body, and the Holy Grail, from the legends of King Arthur, that gives nourishment to the soul, are not as improbable to believe as you might think, when you listen to the messages sent to you in dreams.

When members of a family die, they are no longer concerned, with having to provide for their own earthly needs, and so they provide for the needs of family and friends, on the earth plane.

It is therefore advisable, to keep a record of what happens, and during this six week period and you will be reassured, that your loved ones in spirit are looking after you.

The same situation, also applies around our individual birthdays, and so again, it is wise to make a note, of any opportunities happening around this period.

So do not say each morning, "It was just a dream", but instead spare a moment to write down the gist of the dream, as it maybe your higher self, analysing the events of the previous day, and providing valuable insight into the happenings of the day, or it may be;

Loved Ones, in spirit, trying to alert you to an opportunity, or it may be, your higher self, indicating an opportunity for personal growth.

CHAPTER ONE

Child's Play

I have found that the messages that we receive in dreams can be roughly categorized in four ways: Health/diet, Finance/career, love/relationships, and personal growth. These four categories also tap into the motivation and resilience of the human spirit that fortifies the individual by providing them with a vision of something beyond their immediate experiences, whether it is being reunited with loved ones, or publishing an inspired piece of work as so poignantly illustrated, in the work by Viktor Frankl, "Man's Search for Meaning". It is that "something", which gives the individual, the necessary strength to carry on, and a sense of something greater than themselves.

And even though, we may not be subjected, to the same type of horrific situations, our dreams serve the same purpose. They inspire us to keep going when everything and everyone seem to be against us, and sometimes it is a struggle, to just keep our head above water.

During these difficult times, we sometimes become so overwhelmed by situations, that we are unable to hear the guidance of the dream voice, which is offering solutions, to what may seem to be insurmountable problems, and yet, there is an unbelievably easy way to break this spiritual drought.

Simply ask for an answer!

Before retiring for the night, arm yourself with a pen and pad and place them on your bedside table. It is also advisable to have a torch handy, if no bedside lamp is available.

- ❖ Now either write down a specific question or ask a specific question of your higher self, which is your connection to, Divine energy. Ask only one question each night, or you will confuse the answers.
- ❖ Ask to be given a statement in a dream, giving the exact answer to the question.
- ❖ Ask to remember the statement.

Write down the statement that you may get in the middle of the night, because as dreams are fleeting, they can easily be forgotten by the time you wake up in the morning.

Remember, the statement may not be given in the expected context, but it is only the statement that you need pay attention to, not the background information.

We get four or five dreams every night, and although dreams are very vivid at the time, unless we tag them some way, they will have disappeared by morning.

If you do not get the answer to your question the first night, do not become discouraged, as persistence will pay off and if you ask again the second night, you should get the answer.

At the outset, you may have to ask a third night, but after that, information that you seek should come much more easily. Think of it as if you are cracking a code and once you have cracked the code, it is plain sailing for the rest of your life.

Remember that dreams work with symbolic language, and it is only the statement in the dream that you need to pay attention to.

The proof is in the pudding! The following examples, explain this clearly.

A female client, who needed to sell the family home, because of a divorce, felt overwhelmed, by the emotional circumstances, surrounding her situation, asked me for advice. I suggested that she use the, four stage, dream technique mentioned above.

And so, a) she asked to be told in a dream, the number of weeks in which the house would be sold, b) she asked to be given a statement in her dream, giving the exact number of weeks, c) she asked to remember the statement, and d) she had a pen and pad ready, to write down the answer.

Having a pen and pad beside the bed is a very necessary part of the dream process.

This is a demonstration of "Good Will," which is a component of any business transaction, and we are now choosing to make a contract with our higher selves, agreeing to do what is necessary in exchange for the information that we want.

That night, my client got the answer to her question in the following dream. My client dreamed that, she was in conversation, with her older son, who said to her, "Mum, I have chickenpox, but I will be better in six weeks."

As her son did not in fact have chickenpox, the lady realised, that the length of time required for the sale of the house, must be six weeks, and indeed it was. In six weeks, she sold the house.

The time-frame for the recovery from chickenpox, was symbolic of the time-frame for the sale of the house. The symbolism of chickenpox, alluded to the embarrassment that my client had felt, at having her house up for sale, and the uncomfortable, public position, that she had found herself in, a common feeling, amongst those, who are getting divorced.

Indeed, one gentleman had confided in me, that despite wanting a divorce from his partner, he had felt a sense of failure, in the eyes of society.

I had reassured him, that sometimes it takes more courage to get a divorce, than to stay in an unhappy marriage.

The dream symbolism of her son as the messenger represented "the child within", which needed help.

We have all contained within each of us, the mother, father, child aspect of our personality, which can manifest at certain times and in certain situations and influence how we think and feel as well as how we act.

The child/parent relationship we experienced growing up, will have a significant effect on the inner child that we possess as adults and will influence how we respond to situations and circumstances, which we feel, we have no control over. This is because, as children, we were aware of the disappointment that our behaviour sometimes caused, when we failed to live up to, the expectations of our parents. And as adults we also try to live up to the expectations, of the parent within.

As my client came from a cultural background, where divorce was forbidden, the shame and guilt that she felt about her decision to get a divorce, weighed heavily on her shoulders, and increased her sense of embarrassment. Although my client had two sons, the son who was more concerned with his self-image, appeared in her dream to illustrate how her ego, was affected by the situation, and her concern for the opinions of others.

In an attempt to lessen my client's feelings of guilt and embarrassment, I decided to share with her a very valuable piece of advice that I had received from a priest, many years previously..

The advice is profound in its simplicity. "If people are not paying your bills, why would you care what they think?"

Another example of how to use this dream technique to bypass the ego, which is that part of the personality that needs to be brought under control,_— or its need for self-gratification, may cause serious problems for the dreamer,_— is illustrated by the circumstances of another client, who also had her house on the market for sale.

This client was getting quite anxious, as time was slipping away with no reasonable offers having been made, and as she had inspected a prospective property, that she was keen on buying, she was in danger of self-sabotage, in her haste to buy the other property.

She confided in me, that her intention was to secure a "Bridging loan," to purchase this property, as she felt that, she would not find another property, which would appeal to her as much. As a "Bridging loan", can be a very costly experience, I managed, with difficulty, to persuade my client, not to rush into making a decision, until she had first consulted her dreams, as to the wisdom of her decision. I suggested that she use the technique mentioned earlier, and she reluctantly, and with much scepticism, agreed to do this.

The following day, when the client phoned me, and told me that she had indeed managed to receive a dream, but was unable to make sense of the information, I asked her to share her dream with me, so that I could perhaps provide insight for her. The client said that she felt somewhat embarrassed by the contents of the dream, but, I reassured her that dreams often use dramatic, or confronting symbolism, to get our attention and not to feel embarrassed, as the symbolism used in the dream, is simply something that she could relate to.

The client, a well to do, lady, from a middle-class background, told me that her dream had taken place in her bedroom. She had dreamed that she had been lying on a huge, king-size, four-poster bed. Lying, at the bottom, of the bed, on the left-hand side, was an old lady, who was asleep, and lying on the bottom right-hand side of the bed, was a handsome young man. In the dream, the handsome young man, began to suck her toes, gradually working his way up her leg, making her feel very hot and flustered. So much so, that she was forced to shout out," Stop! It's not the right time." And then, she suddenly, woke up.

I explained to my client, that the four-poster bed symbolised the plum piece of real estate, that she currently owned, and which allowed her to occupy a good financial position in the real estate market, asset-wise. The old lady in the dream, who was asleep, represented the wisdom, or intuitive side, of her nature, which was unavailable to her at this point in time. She was allowing her desires, or self indulgence, represented by the handsome young man who was sucking her toes, to cloud her judgment.

I explained that the feelings of being hot and flustered were an indication of how she would feel if she took out the "Bridging loan", and her statement, or shout of "Stop! Its not the right time" was the advice that she had sought from her dream that was warning her, against making a serious error of judgment.

The side of the bed, occupied by the individuals in her dream, was also significant, as the left hand side, represents intuition and the right hand side, represents the mind and logic.

Also, as my client is a ten in numerology, (see section on numerology) which is composed of the one, a masculine symbol of business and the market place, as well as that, of someone who likes to be in control of situations, and the zero which represents the feminine intuitive aspect, both characters in her dream represented both parts of her own personality and indicated that her initial judgment of the situation was unbalanced, indicated by the old lady being asleep.

Pythagoras the proclaimed father of mathematics, was also a philosopher, and was led to the conclusion that certain numerical formulae formed the basis of each individual's personality and behaviour, which we call Numerology.

By understanding these formulae, we develop better self-awareness, and consequently a more balanced and harmonious out look on life, as well as, adding another dimension, to the interpretation of dreams.

Our life-path number, according to Pythagoras, is the driving force behind our aspirations and our ability to achieve.

The more knowledge we possess, the more symbolism is at the disposal of the dreaming mind, and hence the more detailed and elaborate the dreams that we experience.

This client had almost sabotaged herself through her lack of self- discipline and through indulging her desire for immediate self- gratification, from her need to control what was happening in her life, instead of allowing events to run their natural course.

And of course as this particular client who is under the influence of the planet Jupiter, being a Sagittarius astrological sign, was about to sabotage the financial success that is her birth-right under these auspicious influences, (see section on astrological star signs).

As a consequence of the advice given to her in her dreams, my client waited for her home to sell, which it did a short time later, providing her with an even greater windfall than she had expected, leading to the opportunity of buying a more appealing property than the one she had so desperately wanted earlier.

How many times do we find that the disappointment we felt at the failure of what we desperately wanted to happen at a particular time in our lives turns to gratitude later, as we realise how close we came, to sabotaging our opportunities in life?

Our birth-right, under particular planetary influences, will often be a source of surprise, as well as one of success, as was discovered by another client of mine, a Pisces and self- proclaimed bachelor. Pisces is the only other star sign, which is influenced directly by the planet Jupiter, and so Pisceans are also lucky, when it comes to financial opportunities.

The client asked me to explain the following dream that he had.

In his dream, he was in deep conversation with a mixed group of people, when he noticed a large, white dog, near by.

Suddenly the white dog spotted my client, and ran over towards the group, wagging its tail, as it approached my client.

The dog seemed to be very pleased to see my client, and fondled him, and although the dog was very friendly towards him, it would not go to any one else, no matter how much they encouraged it to do so.

I explained to my client that, as a friendly white dog approaching someone in a dream, indicates a business opportunity, or an early marriage, depending on the circumstances surrounding the dreamer at the time, I told my client that a business opportunity was around him at the moment, that only he, would benefit from, which was why, in the dream, the large, friendly, white dog, refused to go to anyone else.

Some time later, the client confided in me that, at the time of the dream, there had been a rental, investment property, available for him to buy, that had been unprofitable for its previous owner, but despite this, because of his dream, he bought it and he has managed to make it, into a very successful investment.

These two clients will always be successful in business, as the lucky planet Jupiter, which influences their individual star signs, will provide guaranteed opportunities in the material world, which their dreams will always steer them towards, so it would be a good investment of their time to pay attention to messages that they receive in dreams.

Reference to the story of the "Ten talents", in the Holy Bible, would not go amiss here, as it describes how, we are stewards of the talents that we are born with, and that we will be held to account, as to how wisely we managed them.

It would also seem from this that any skills and talents which one develops during a particular life-time, will lead to, the development of even more opportunities, during successive lifetimes.

CHAPTER TWO

Premonitions

Premonitions of an impending death, are a common occurrence, amongst Irish families and delight, at recounting dreams and horror stories, were one of the favourite past times of my family, when we were growing up. We would sit around a roaring, coal fire, on freezing, winter nights, with the lights out and the flickering firelight casting strange, distorted shapes, on the walls, and ceiling, as we whispered, in slow, dramatic tones, jumped at any strange noises that came out of the darkness.

My father told us, that he had heard the call of the Banshee, just before his maternal grandmother died and my older sister, Colette also claimed, that she too, had heard the Banshee, just before my father's brother died.

The Banshee is a little fairy woman, who cries, as she combs her long, white, silvery hair, in the moonlight, warning of an impending death in a family.

In Irish culture, it is believed, that certain sounds also precede a death, in particular families, and one of these sounds, that of the "Death Watch Beetle", ticking loudly throughout the house, was heard by both my brother Chris and myself, before the sudden death of a priest, who was a second cousin.

Dreams however, are the usual way in which we become aware of an impending death.

Abraham Lincoln, a former American President, had a dream, in which he received a warning of his own impending death.

In his dream, he had heard a woman crying, in the White House, and he followed the sound to a room, where a coffin was on display.

When he asked the woman,' What has happened here?', she replied

"The president is dead!".

When he looked into the coffin, he saw his own body lying there.

Two weeks later, he was assassinated, while at the Opera.

Before my grandmother died, my aunt had dreamed that she and my grandmother were walking together, along a country lane, when they came to a style.

In the dream, my grandmother climbed over the style and my aunt made to follow her, but my grandmother turned to my aunt and said,

"I have to do this alone",

Then, as my aunt watched, my grandmother disappeared into a mist.

A few months later, my grandmother died.

This dream also reminds us that, death is a rite of passage, which has to be undertaken alone.

However like all predictions and prophecies, it is only after an event takes place, that verification can happen and the same applies to our dreams.

We can only know that we have had a premonition, after the event has happened, and that is another good reason, to record dreams.

Also, the people who appear in our dreams, often represent some one else, but there is some type of connection to the person or circumstance that is happening around the dreamer at the time of the dream to the person in the dream.

Our dreamscape will use images that we are familiar with, to warn us, of an event.

The country lane in my aunt's dream was reminiscent of the place where she grew up and her dream was showing her that her mother, (my grandmother), was now going home.

When my grandmother did come to die, and her family was gathered around her bedside, she described to those at her bedside, the vision that she had of her husband James, coming up the garden path, to meet her.

And, with her dying breath, she described a vision of a white bird flying around the room.

Images in dreams, of attending a funeral, may herald a death, or a plume of black smoke, from a chimney, in the same way that the Vatican uses the image of black smoke to signal the death of a Pope. The dreaming mind will use images that the dreamer is familiar with.

Indeed, this same image, of dark smoke, coming out of a chimney, alerted me, to the impending death of my mother, many years ago.

As my father had died many years before her, my mother, had become the head of the large Catholic family, which I had been born into, and because she was such a committed Catholic, my dreamscape likened her death, to that of a Pope.

Premonitions however, are not always about sadness and tragedy; they are also about joyous occasions, like a pregnancy, or the birth of a child, or an unexpected encounter with a special person, or even a sudden windfall.

My mother had a premonition about a successful business deal that my father was about to conclude.

She had dreamed that she and my father were waltzing around the room together.

The dream had surprised my mother, as, although my father was an accomplished dancer, my mother had two left feet. However, in the dream, there was a feeling of happiness and she knew that something good was about to happen.

To dream of dancing, is an indication of some unexpected good fortune.

And indeed, the successful business deal, enabled my father to retire comfortably, and he was able to enjoy his remaining years, without any financial worries, as well as, leaving my mother in a position, to do the same.

It is unfortunate however, that we only tend to remember more vividly, those events that have had a negative impact upon our lives.

Dream exploration can help develop, close-knit, family ties, as well as helping to develop intuition in children, and is a useful past time, that is engaged in, by indigenous people, to help children accept the natural rhythms of life.

The Seneca Indian tribe of North America, like many indigenous cultures, worked intimately with their dreams, looking for hidden meanings, that might indicate the health of the dreamer, as well as using their dreams, to go on vision quests, to benefit the whole tribe.

Indeed, when I finally became disillusioned with my Catholic upbringing, I had a dream in which I saw a group of nuns, who appeared to be panic stricken, at the sudden realisation that their belief system had been completely destroyed, and one of the nuns asked "What are we to believe in now?"

In the dream, a voice answered, "Believe in Seneca."

At the time of this dream, I was unaware of who Seneca was, and I assumed that it was a person, and possibly of Greek origin, and was unsure of what I was supposed to do, but assumed that all would be made clear eventually, which it was.

Many years after my research began, into the dreaming mind, and the benefit for the individual, I had a dream in which I was asked, "If you were to take something with you when you die, what would you take?" and without hesitation I replied, "The Dreams".

When I woke up, I believed that, in the dream, I was being asked, to nominate a talent which, I would choose, to take with me into my next reincarnation.

Through my research into different belief systems about dreams, I found that the belief system of the North American, Seneca, Indian tribe, was most closely related, to my dream experiences and I knew then, that my dreams were what I could depend on, to sustain me.

Discussing dreams with family members, is a good habit for parents to adopt, as the time spent analysing family dreams, will alert parents, to problems with their children, that they are not consciously aware of, such as bullying at school, possible depression, unhealthy associations, as well as dangerous activities that their children may be involved in.

I always encouraged my sons, to take their dreams seriously, and when they were young, we would spend hours together, discussing the possible meanings of their dreams.

I considered this to be quality, family-time, spent together, as it gave everyone a chance to be the centre of attention and have their say. As my sons became older, they would often get me to analyse, not only their dreams, but the dreams of their friends as well.

One young man, who was a friend of the family, asked me about a strange dream that he had, just after beginning employment at a local club.

He told me, that he had a dream of standing on top of a cliff, in conversation with another employee. The young man told me, that in his dream, he could see a ferry, down in the water below the cliff and there also seemed to be a mist around them.

The ferryman in Greek mythology ferried the dead, over the river Styx, to the underworld and a mist, in Celtic mythology, usually represents someone passing over, into the other side, a death, I felt, was imminent.

I explained to the young man, that because he had honed his natural skills of intuition, over the years, he was aware, of the proximity of the veil, which exists between the worlds, and so his dream was a premonition, of an impending death.

Later that same week, the young man told me that the employee, whom he had been speaking to in his dream, had died of a sudden heart attack, a couple of days after he had the dream.

I believe that the young man, had been given this information in his dream, to prepare him for what was about to happen, as he was only seventeen, and a sudden death, is often more difficult to comprehend, at that age.

Many people have the ability, to use their dreams, to access this type of information, but to understand, the meaning of dreams, careful, regular study of dreams, is necessary.

Dream interpretation is like polishing furniture, it has to be done regularly, to maintain the shine, and because it also requires discipline to do this, one needs to feel motivated enough to make it a way of life.

So many times, clients leave me after a reading, feeling enthusiastic about recording their dreams, only to tell me upon our next meeting, that their determination soon petered out.

As the old proverb says;

"The road to hell is paved with good intentions"

We are all "Shamans", on a vision quest, to help either ourselves, or our families and yet, although we are constantly bombarded with information in our dreams, to help us in our quests, we dismiss this free, vital information, so quickly.

Another reason, however, why a person may choose, not to remember their dreams, is a fear of knowing what the future holds, because of unpleasant experiences in the past.

Many unsettling visions of future events earlier in the life of one client, had dissuaded her, from harnessing her dreams and visions, in a more constructive way.

One of the more distressing dreams that she had, was of a small white coffin, being carried into the house, through the back door of the family home, as it was unable to be carried in, through the front door.

A week later, one of her sisters, got knocked off her bicycle, and died shortly after. Her sister was fifteen at the time.

When the white coffin was brought to the house, as in the dream, it had to be taken in through the back door, as it would not fit through the front door.

My client had felt somehow responsible for the tragedy, as she had a premonition of it in her dream, and so began to block out other messages in her dreams.

Often, people who have premonitions about unpleasant and distressing future events, feel that they, are in some way responsible, for these events, similar to the guilt often experienced by people who survive a tragedy, where others may have perished.

I try to reassure these people, that their dreams are preparing them for what is going to happen, and that they personally, in no way contribute to the situation, other than being privy to the event before it happens, and so are able to better deal with the situation and also, are better able to help others, who may not be as resilient as the dreamer, as was the case of this particular dreamer.

The lady, a five in numerology (see numerology section), who, as well as having the usual, exceptional qualities, associated with this life-path number, also possesses the qualities of medium ship, another trait associated with this number, which embodies the five senses.

Her life-path number, means that she has innumerable resources at her disposal, and part of her life-path lesson, is to use these resources, by engaging with others and not hoarding her skills and isolating herself from others. Practical use of her limitless knowledge is required.

Friends and family members of those who are a life path five, frequently complain of feeling left out, as the life-path five individuals, internalise situations, rather than discussing them with others, and consequently, misunderstandings often arise.

The fact that the lady's astrological sign, is that of Taurus the bull, which imbues those associated with this sign, with a sensible, and reliable approach to life in general, and a good-natured disposition, that others can depend on in times of crisis, meant that she was well suited, to be the one chosen by the universe, to be prepared in advance, for what was about to happen and so enabling her, to help other family members.

Often, if we have honed our intuitive nature, we are able to help others, whether it is close friends, or family members, or even others that we may have contact with, in a casual way, through the information that we receive in our dreams.

I was fortunate enough to be able to do this recently, when I encountered some one, while I was on holiday in New Zealand, the "Land of the Long White Cloud".

I had popped into a, "New Age" shop, in the town of Napier, looking for a gift for one of my sons, and found myself in conversation with another customer.

We began discussing dreams and as we did so, the lady asked if I would do her numerology, as I had mentioned how accurate I had found it to be, regarding personality traits, and as an indicator, of the years of significant change, in our lives, as well as, influencing our dreams.

As I began to do the lady's numerology chart, I realised, that the numbers in her chart, indicating the types of changes that were around her at the moment, corresponded to the dream that I had dreamed, the night before, and that my dream, was in fact, about her situation, and the opportunities, that from a sense of fear, she had let slip through her fingers.

In my dream, someone had dropped two, or three, copper coins, that had landed, "heads up" on the ground, and in my dream, I had bent down and. I had picked up the dropped coins and I had given them back, to the person, who had dropped them.

The lady whose numerology chart, that I had just completed, had two, nine year periods, in her chart, under the number, 5.

As the number two, and the number three combined is five, and the number of coins, that I had picked up from the floor in my dream, indicated the number 5, I realised that this lady was at a crossroads in her life, where she needed to make a very careful decision.

The number 5 in numerology indicates a difficult period in one's life, where arguments prevail and where a physical movement, away from a situation, such as a divorce, may be necessary. The dropped coins in my dream, suggested, that for a second time, this lady was letting the opportunity slip through her fingers, to move away from an unhappy situation, and change her life for the better.

The fact that the coins were "heads up", indicated, that it was the right time to do this, and that everything would work out, in everyone's best interest.

I explained to the lady in question, that her future opportunities were dependent on her courage to follow through, on opportunities available now, and that by using messages received in her dreams, she would have all the reassurance needed to do just that.

As this particular lady is a, life-path number ten, I have no doubt, that she will successfully navigate, any emotional turmoil caused by other people's interference, by listening to the promptings from her inner self, and messages sent to her, in her dreams.

The lady had felt enormously relieved by what I told her, as she had felt in her heart, she had short changed herself, by not having the courage earlier, to follow her intuition, because of fear of the unknown, but now with reassurance from her dreams, she would do so.

One of the most important, as well as, saddest messages, which I ever received in my dream, was for a very dear friend of mine, who developed breast cancer, and who, despite seeking every available treatment, sadly passed away, leaving a husband and three young children.

My dear friend asked me, if I had had any dreams about her, as she was aware that her time was quickly running out.

I was aware of how distressed my friend was, about leaving her three young children and because of whom, she had so bravely, undergone such rigorous cancer treatment in the past, and so using the technique mentioned earlier, I asked to be given a message for her in my dream.

Surprisingly, the message that I received for my friend, in my dreams, was not about her children, as I had expected, as they, were her greatest concern, but about herself.

I told her, that I was told in my dream, that she would be ready when the time came for her to die, and that her father, would be there to meet her.

I told her that I had seen her dancing down the steps of a wide staircase, and that her father was at the bottom, waiting to meet her.

Going down stairs in a dream, can represent going down into your subconscious, to access information, that is not, at this point in time, readily available, to the conscious mind, but going down stairs, can also indicate being unlucky in your affairs, just as passing up a stair, can indicate that good fortune will attend the dreamer.

When analysing a dream, it is important to take into account, all that is happening around the dreamer, at that point in time, and that will provide insight, as to the correct meaning of the dream.

Sadly, I explained to my dear friend, that I didn't know why, she would be ready to die when the time came, but that she would be ready, as dancing symbolises being in touch with the rhythms of life.

Six months later, my dear friend rang, and told me, that she was ready to die now, as the cancer had travelled into her brain and she had gone blind.

And sadly, two weeks later, my dear friend died.

I believe the message that was given to me was to help my friend, face the fear of death and assure her, that she would be reunited, with her loved ones, who were already in spirit.

Also, as the message for my dear friend informed her, that it was her father, who would be there to meet her, and not her mother, whom she was closest to, she was reassured, as to the authenticity of the dream. I had known, that my friend, who was on the life-path 6 number was close to her mother, as all on this life-path number are, and yet contrary to expectation, it would be her father, who helped her cross over, and not her mother.

I believe that this gave my friend the reassurance that she needed, that the soul would continue on after death.

This need for reassurance that death is not "the end" is often given to the dying, through vivid dreams, as they wait, for life to be extinguished.

CHAPTER THREE

Fortitude

As well as death, there are other major hurdles in life, that we have to overcome, and information from our dreams, arm us with the necessary skills, to deal with these.

An unexpected redundancy, from the local High school, where I had been teaching, and a one way ticket, from my father to Australia, to find a husband and a better way of life, opened up a new set of challenges for me.

When my second son, was about a year old, I got bitten by a spider!

The doctors, believed at the time, that it might have been a white tail spider, that often has nasty consequences for the victim, but as it happened while I was asleep, no one could be sure.

I had simply woken up one morning, to find a red line of poison, running up my left arm, from the base of my left thumb, into my lymph glands.

I was misdiagnosed initially, and a couple of days later, my finger tips began to turn black.

After this, I was admitted to St. Vincent's Hospital, Short Stay ward in Sydney, where a condition of scleroderma with a rheumatoid arthritis factor, was diagnosed and a course of treatment recommended.

It seems that spider bites, can activate a dormant illness, and as one of my aunts, had been crippled with rheumatoid arthritis, it appeared, that I had a pre-disposition for the disease and the spider bite was the catalyst to ignite it.

The prognosis for my condition was one of doom and gloom, with the likelihood of being crippled and in a wheel chair, like my aunt, in thirteen years, and this had a profound effect on the dynamics of my family life.

My relationship with my younger son became difficult, and eventually in sheer frustration at his rebellious behaviour, I demanded to know, why he was behaving so badly.

It turned out, that he had felt neglected by my inability to continue performing my usual family duties, of caring for him and his brother, as my hands were too painful to use and the skin of my fingers, would stick to surfaces, forcing me to wear gloves and so limited what I could actually do, around the family home.

His response shocked me, but at the same time, gave me a chance to redeem myself.

Absolutely shocked and horrified by his outburst of, "You don't care about us, you do nothing for us", I realized that, not only did my condition have such a huge impact on my life, but it had turned my younger son, into a very angry little man.

It is common in families, to find that the illness of one family member has a huge impact, on the lives of the rest of the family, and a grieving process, follows any diagnosis of prolonged ill health. The fear of loss of enjoyment of life, as well as potential loss of career opportunities contributes to feelings of insecurity and a re-negotiation of the status quo is inevitable.

The personal consequences of an illness, often leaves the affected party, in a state of numbness, as they try to come to terms with the unexpected situation, and life begins to be lived on a, day to day, basis only.

It is not surprising that this self absorption with the situation, leads to a breakdown in communication between family members.

After this incident with my younger son, I realized that I needed to stop feeling sorry for myself and get serious about getting better.

One of the change agents in my life was learning to read Tarot cards. It constituted one, of the many learning themes, I undertook, whilst at University. I found it an interesting exercise in the power of the mind, as well as, the power of suggestion.

Tarot cards, although frowned upon by many people, are in their most basic form, simply picture cards, that appeal to the imagination.

Like most things, they are neither good nor bad of themselves, it is the interpretation by the individual, which projects a negative, or positive response, to them, as well as for what purpose they are used.

This is true even of the Holy Bible, where unscrupulous individuals, may manipulate the meaning, for unholy purposes.

I found however, that learning to read the Tarot and the feelings of guilt aroused in me, because of a very religious upbringing, in Northern Ireland, resurrected an old nightmare, which I had suffered from as a child, of being chased by the devil, down to hell.

When running away from something in a dream, we are being alerted to a situation that we are refusing to address, in our waking lives. We need to have the courage to turn and face whatever it is, that we are running away from. As a consequence, what we have the courage to confront in the dream state, will translate to having the courage, to face situations in our waking lives.

In my case, it was all about accessing personal power, and about my refusal to use my personal power, to help myself, instead of always being dependent on others. Also about pleasing others, at the expense of me and being, the good girl, an unfortunate failing of those like me, who are born under life-path seven, in numerology.

Severe consequences, can befall life-path seven individuals, who fail to take personal control of their lives, instead, foolishly trusting that being honest themselves, others will be honest with them and treat them with fairness.

This reluctance, to stand up to the rigors of life and take charge of situations, will have a negative impact on others, and not just the individual themselves.

One client, who is also a life-path seven, asked me to explain a recurring nightmare, which she had suffered from since childhood.

This charming lady, had spent her childhood on a farm, where a deep well was located, at the front of the property.

In her nightmare, the lady was aware of a man, living at the bottom of the well, but she was too terrified to look into the well, as she was frightened that the man might grab hold of her.

This particular nightmare is a classic example of the denial of the masculine, rational side of the female nature, which prompts the individual, to look at situations objectively and deal with them in an appropriate way.

The image of the farm represents success in business. The image of the well, represents intuition. The man represents the masculine aspect of the female nature, which helps her to achieve success in the material world, while the feminine aspect of a woman's nature, gives birth to creativity. The fear of the man down the well indicates the dreamer's fear of combining her intuitive nature, with her innate shrewdness and tenacity, to achieve the personal success, which she is capable of, as an individual who is born under the astrological sign of Cancer.

Unfortunately, through years of neglect, caused by an acceptance of the status quo in the society that she is from, and without any challenge to the prescribed roles of that society, a distorted and confused judgment has been made, about what is acceptable, and what is expected and this has led, to an inability to develop self awareness and an understanding of herself, as an individual.

And so, a consequence of years of ignoring this vital aspect of her nature, this softly spoken woman, has found herself in an unhappy marriage, but from years of habit, of not questioning assumptions and turning a blind eye to situations, she lacks, the willpower, to change the circumstances of her life and so has perhaps, inadvertently, set up a pattern of behaviour, that will influence the attitude of her children, to their future partners.

In her book, "The Wounded Woman", Linda Schierse Leonard explores the father/daughter relationship and the importance of the father, as the first masculine figure that a daughter relates to, and the influence that this has on a woman's attitude to the masculine within herself, as well as to the masculine in society, in general.

Similarly, just as in a daughter's outer life, if her father provided a positive role model in waking life, the image will be likewise in the dreaming state. However, if the role model has not been a positive one, conflicts that may arise within the self, and to patriarchal society in general that need to be addressed, will manifest, within the dream state.

However, although change becomes increasingly difficult as we get older, it is not too late for change for this life-path seven individual, as those born under this life-path have a natural, spiritual protection around them, like a built in warning system, that alerts them to any pitfalls looming up ahead, however, they do need to listen, to the promptings from the inner self.

One young man, who is also a life path seven, came into contact with his feminine side, the female aspect of the male, in a dream, which he found very challenging and so he asked me to explain the dream for him.

In his dream he was going up the stairs towards his bedroom, when he found himself standing outside the door of a toilet that was located just before his bedroom.

There, he met a woman, whose face was half eastern and half western.

He continued up the stairs to his bedroom, but found on entering the room that a cat had been in there and defecated all over the floor and he felt disgusted by the sight.

At the time of the dream, the young man, who had a latent homosexual nature, which had been suppressed for years, by his strong, Catholic upbringing was now being alerted by his subconscious, that there was conflict within his psyche, by the denial of his true nature?

The woman, whose face represented two opposing cultural belief systems, illustrated the conflicting feelings within the young man, as to how he should present himself, to the world.

His disgust at the cat defecating in his bedroom was an indication of how he felt about his intuitive, feminine nature, intruding into his consciousness, as he knew that it would be only a matter of time, before his innermost fears, of being found out, would be realized, and there would be unpleasant, repercussions in family life.

The goal of becoming a whole person is to be in relationship with all aspects of the personality, so that any suppressed aspect, does not surface at an unexpected and inappropriate moment and provide a nasty shock for the individual.

Eventually, after many, years of soul searching, the young man finally accepted his true sexual nature and now lives a happier and more fulfilling life.

In numerology, seven is considered to be the transformer and as such, those individuals born into this life path number are able to change karmic patterns of family behaviour as they have an internal fortitude that helps them to survive whatever trials that life may throw at them.

The negative aspect of life path seven individuals, can lead to a refusal, to take the necessary action, to change their current circumstances, hoping to avoid pain at any cost and instead of being more focused in their lives, and having more self discipline, they scatter their talents.

Marilyn Monroe is an example of a life path seven individual, who failed to read the warning signs of imminent destruction and change course accordingly.

She died at the age of 36, the age of maturity, when we should view life, from a more mature perspective and not, in the self-indulgent style, of the adolescent.

Each decade of our lives, brings with it, different opportunities, than the previous decade and these in turn, also bring other responsibilities.

Throughout our lives, we learn that the survival of our relationships and the integrity of our family, depend on us behaving in a certain way. We learn what others expect and want of us and what we need to do, to be able to function appropriately, in both family life and the wider society.

However, we need to learn how to do this appropriately, by setting boundaries, so that we can be who we are, in our relationships, rather than who others wish us to be, need us to be, expect us to be and we must allow others to do the same.

One does not get their needs met, at the expense of the other.

The tarot card of The Devil, also represents bad habits, of giving in to others and surrendering your power, to keep the peace, in order to have your immediate needs met.

At the other extreme of bad habits is the person who, takes all the time and allowing this to happen, is not in the best interests of either party.

The following dream that a client asked my opinion about illustrates the point.

The client told me that her five year old son had a dream in which a little fat pig was chasing him, but he wasn't unduly worried about what was happening in the dream.

I had told her that the pig represented the little boy himself and that he was being 'pig-headed' and that by running away from the pig, he was refusing to acknowledge that he was being self indulgent in his behaviour. His dream was warning him, that he needed to take his behaviour more seriously and address the issue now, or there may be future consequences for his behaviour.

Running away from anything in a dream, indicates that we are running away from an aspect of our own personality, which needs to be integrated, to enable us to function properly and utilize our full potential as an individual.

As the young man is under the astrological sign of Virgo, an earth sign, and like all earth signs, he is often tempted to push boundaries to see how far he can go; the dream about the pig was showing him that he had reached his limit.

Before developing my intuition and honing my psychic talents, I used to have a reoccurring dream, where I was being chased by a golden horse.

In the dream, I had my two sons, by either hand, and I was running as fast as I could, from the golden horse, as I was frightened, that it would hurt my two sons.

Eventually I ran into a tent with my two sons, hoping that we would be safe there, but the golden horse came into the tent and found me.

As the horse represents the power within the individual, and gold represents the ultimate in spirituality, my dream was alerting me to my reluctance to develop my connection to Divine energy, by listening to, and utilizing, the messages that I was receiving in my dreams, because of my concern, of how it would impact upon my children.

The tent represented the situation that I eventually found myself in, because of my divorce, which lacked financial security, and so finally forced me, to develop my talent for prophecy, inherited from my grandmother, whose premonitions and dreaming skills, I was well aware of, as a child.

Indeed, once I began to use my dreaming skills constructively, I no longer gave away my power to other people and although situations often still, fill me with trepidation, once I check in with my higher self through my dreams, I will give it my best shot, such as Bungy-jumping, in Queenstown, New Zealand, on my 62nd birthday.

CHAPTER FOUR

Trust Factor

I found that the symbolism of the tarot, had a significant influence on my dream landscape, and a few years later when my marriage began to founder, it was the image in the tarot of, "The Fool" and his dog, which represented taking a leap of faith, along with other messages, that helped me to navigate the perilous waters of divorce.

Divorce is always a traumatic situation for everyone involved, and the vested interests of either party, can muddy the waters to the extent that reason and common sense, no longer prevail.

Sadly, it is usually the children who suffer most, as they seem to end up as helpless pawns in the divorce proceedings, with each parent claiming that they are doing what is best for the children, but in reality, bruised egos and financial concerns can often be the driving force behind any claims made.

I did not want to fall into the same traps, which others got caught up in, and so I asked to be told in a dream, what I should do in the best interests of my children, as I knew that we were both loving parents.

I was horrified to be told in my dream, to allow each child to choose the parent that they would prefer to live with.

My first reaction was, "what if they do not want to live with me, I will be lonely?"

However, we cannot pick and choose, the part of our dreams, that we will accept advice from, as there will be a consequence to pay, and so, despite many objections from others, I asked both my sons, to decide which parent they would prefer to be based with, believing that it was an acceptable way of dealing with the situation.

The wisdom of my decision to follow this advice, and how it impacted in a positive way with my children, was demonstrated in a dream, which my younger son had, after the divorce.

My son told me that he had dreamed that, his father and I were in a plane crash, but that we had both walked away unhurt, and that he and his brother were alright, because they had been in Hawaii at the time.

I explained to my son, that the plane represented the marriage between his father and me and that it was no longer working successfully.

And just as the plane had crashed in his dream, because it was unable to continue flying because of some kind of problem, his father and I were unable to continue in the relationship that we were in, as it was no longer functioning properly.

I also explained that in his subconscious mind, he was aware of what was happening and so the situation was coming into his conscious mind through his dreams.

And I explained, that he was also aware, that no matter what happened between his father and me, he and his brother would enjoy life even more, despite the situation, which was indicated by the image of Hawaii, an enjoyable place to be.

Also, the fact that neither his father nor I, were injured in the plane crash, and that we were able to walk away unhurt, reassured my son that the crash of the marriage would not prevent his father and I from getting on with our lives.

This dream that my son shared with me, convinced me of the importance of teaching children to explore the meaning of their dreams, so that, in situations where they feel that they have no control over the decisions made by others, a sense of security can be achieved through dream exploration.

I feel that the use of dreams, to help children understand situations that are happening around them, is an invaluable tool, to provide emotional and psychological well being.

I believe, that the decision to give our sons the choice of deciding which parent they would prefer to be based with, contributed to the Hawaii aspect of the dream.

Each child chose the parent which best suited their needs.

I believe that my ex- husband may have agreed to the proposal, because I think, that as I was still suffering a great deal of pain from my condition, he believed, that both sons would prefer to stay with him.

However, our younger son chose to stay with his father, but our older son chose to stay with me.

As a consequence, each child had the undivided attention and perks, which are usually the prerogative of an only child.

I do admit that I did have reservations about separating the two boys, but again, my dreams gave me the reassurance needed, that it was the best situation for both of them.

I had a dream in which I saw two young trees, that were growing too close together and although the smaller of the two trees, had lots of fruit on the tree, some of the fruit had fallen on the ground and been squashed.

The tree represented the tree of life, and fruit on the tree, represented the talents and potential opportunities, which my younger son had been born with. The fruit, that had fallen and been squashed, indicated that some of his opportunities, or talents, had not been utilized to their best advantage..

Perhaps being born under the sporty, Astrological sign of Virgo, he should have been allowed to play soccer, instead of football, and then perhaps he would have become a famous soccer player, like Gorgie Best. Who knows what his missed opportunities were, but at least now, with the divorce, he would be able to shine in his own right and not feel overshadowed, by his more extroverted, older brother.

Indeed my younger son had been in trouble at school for misbehaving, but I knew that he was not the problem; it was the situation between his father and me, that he was reacting to, and later after the divorce, with encouragement and help from his grandfather, he shone academically at school, and received several, outstanding- achievement awards.

My younger son's dream had allowed me to see, that everyone would emotionally survive the collapse of the marriage and provided reassurance about the decisions being made.

As for my older son, one of his friends once remarked that he was lucky to have his mother all to himself.

This comment is reminiscent of the Oedipus complex, that children are often accused of suffering from, because of an attachment to a particular parent and which often manifests, as a reluctance to leave home, when they are older, to establish their own families.

It is a common occurrence in families that a son, often replaces the father, in the affections of the mother, causing internal family conflict, just as a daughter, often replaces the mother, in the affections of the father, and this too, can cause a great deal of unhappiness.

In dreams, we are often alerted to this problem, in a simple and straight forward way.

One young lady, in her mid twenties, who was an avid card player, told me that she had a dream one night, where she was seated at a table, with a group of people playing cards.

She looked at the "hand" that she was holding, only to discover that there were too many Queens, in the deck.

When she asked me to explain the symbolism, I told her that she was competing with her mother, for her father's affection and that it was now time for her, to move out of the family home.

And not long after the dream, she did just that. She found her own place to live, resulting in more harmonious relationships all round.

CHAPTER FIVE

Universal Symbolism

The more extensive the knowledge of symbolism, that the individual possesses, then the more information will be available to the dreaming mind, to illustrate the meaning, or message, being conveyed to the dreamer.

After my divorce, "The Lion", the symbol of courage in the Tarot, began to show up frequently in my dreams. I realized that a huge force was driving me forward and that I needed to be "lion- hearted" to deal with situations.

One dream in particular, forced me to take a long hard look at the reality of my marriage and my relationship with my ex-husband and his family.

In my dream it was night time, which indicates a period when one needs to be careful, as danger could be around.

I was in the driver's seat of a car, which suddenly began to roll down, a long, steep hill.

I tried to stop the car by putting my foot on the brakes, but they were not working.

I was really worried in the dream, that some one would get hurt, by this runaway car, as I could see a beach at the bottom of the hill, where lots of children were playing.

I turned the steering wheel of the car, and managed to slow the car, by steering it into the left-hand, side kerb and gradually, work my way, down the hill and finally it came to rest on the beach with out injuring anyone.

In the dream, everyone cheered as I had successfully managed to get the car safely down to the beach. Parents began to arrive to take their children home, but one little boy seemed to be by himself and was trailing behind one family, who were ignoring him.

He looked at me and said "I am part of this family aren't I?"

In the dream, I felt very sorry for the little boy because I knew that he wasn't part of that family, but he just so wanted to belong.

I woke up from this dream, with an enormous feeling of sadness, as I knew that the little boy was me.

This dream helped me to understand, why the dynamics in my marriage, failed to generate the harmony necessary, for the marriage to succeed.

The difference in cultural background between my ex-husband and me, although quite similar in some ways, was different enough, to lack the cohesion necessary, to make the marriage work.

With the completion of my Masters Degree at University, I had more free time to devote to studying Numerology, and my own Numerology chart, and I found that this helped me to understand my personal strengths, and weaknesses, and the areas of my personality that I needed to work on.

Once I felt confident about using the discipline of Numerology, like the Tarot, I began to 'Read' charts, wherever I went.

People were surprised at the insight their birth-date revealed, about their personality, as well as relationship compatibility, and business prospects. They were also surprised, at how numerology, also, indicated opportunities, that would be available to them, at particular times of their lives.

The ruling number of the individual is an accurate indication, of the type of career and lifestyle, that a person is best suited to and from which they would derive the most personal satisfaction. The accuracy of this belief is illustrated by the following incident involving a, female, teaching colleague. My colleague confided in me, that she had applied for a position that would be a good career move, in the field of education, and was upset at the lack of support for her application, by the school principal, whom she had always considered to be a personal friend, as well as a colleague.

When the teacher had asked the principal for a reference, to support her application, the principal had replied, rather dismissively, "You would not be capable of carrying out this role." and reluctantly, gave her a reference.

As I knew the numerology life path–number, of both the principal and my teaching colleague, I told my colleague that what the principal really meant, was that she could not fulfil that role, as she is a four in numerology and under the astrological sign of Pisces, so her need for security, would have prevented her, from taking on a role that was a new initiative by the Education Department, with no guarantee of its success and continued existence.

My colleague, on the other hand, was born under the astrological sign of Gemini, and a life path of 9 in numerology and so was ambitious, an idealist and loved the mental stimulation that change can bring.

I explained that the role she had applied for was perfect for her, and not to worry about the principal pouring cold water on her hopes, as she would get the job and be in her element, which she did and was tremendously successful.

I enjoyed myself so much analysing the charts of others that the Universe felt it necessary to remind me in a dream, that

Numerology is not a game, but should be taken seriously as it provides a medium for those in spirit, to pass on messages.

In my dream, I had a vision of a very high tower and there were little windows at the top of the tower, from which people were waving hankies at me. I thought, 'they are trying to get my attention and are sending me messages.'

The tower represented spiritual evolution and the windows represented opportunities.

The hankies represented communication and grief, indicating messages being passed on to loved ones, from those in spirit.

Like the tarot, numerology influenced the dreaming state.

When I began to do psychic readings professionally,

I discovered that I could identify messages in my dreams for the clients who came to see me, once I knew their numerology number and their astrological sign.

Sometimes, for up to two weeks, before a client came to see me, I would have a dream about someone I knew and which I of course would record and then, it would become clear who the dream information was meant for, when I did the client's Numerology.

A lady, who came to see me, for a Reading many years ago, had a matter of concern, regarding her business.

When I looked at her Numerology Chart and Star sign, I realized that the dream I had the week before, about one of my younger brothers, was really about her.

I explained to her, how my dream symbolism worked and I told her that my brother who was born under the same astrological sign and had the same life path number as she did, had shown me in a dream that, he had had something hidden, under the bed, that no one knew about, and that it related to a legal matter, and the signing of contracts.

The bed represented intimate or private knowledge that no one else was aware of.

The signing of legal papers indicated the completion of a deal.

The following week the client came back to see me and told me, that she wanted to share with me, how important the message was, that I had given to her.

She said that just before coming to see me, she had been disappointed to have missed out on securing a rental property which she had felt, would be ideal for her business, as a silver-smith.

After coming to see me, she had spent time on the internet looking for a potential rental property and discovered that the rental property, that she had missed out on, was on the market for sale, so she bought the building, from a secret cache, that she had squirreled away over the years.

The message from my dream, had given her the confidence to make the purchase. She was so pleased.

It is important to remember, that the circumstances surrounding the dreamer, at the time of the dream, are important, in relation to the dream material produced by the dreaming mind.

Cultural background, professional circumstances, belief system, age and gender all play a part, in contributing to the dream landscape of the dreamer.

Also, as this lady was a master number eleven, in numerology, the number of good personal, as well as, good business relationships, opportunities available to her would be greater, than those available, to a lesser numerology number. She would have the courage, to take opportunities that those on the life-path of a lesser number, might balk at.

Meanwhile, the more I expanded my psychic awareness, through dreams and numerology and a daily meditation, the more my health improved.

I read everything that I could get my hands on, to do with the power of the mind, positive thinking, herbal remedies, symbolism and dreams and my personal library became a catalogue of a "Whose Who" in the world of healing and natural remedies as well as personal motivation books.

But dreams became my favourite route to good health.

I had a painful condition which I wanted to be rid of and so, dreaming became a way of life for me, with amazing results.

I even began to get information in my dreams about the emotional and physical health of other people, which I began to pass on as well.

This however, was not without its pitfalls, as a few people began to become a bit nervous about being in my company. They believed that I must be reading their minds, and as the information that I was giving them was unsolicited, they began to avoid my company.

In a way this was quite ironic, as my mother used to tell me that I had fallen off the gypsy's cart, because of my ability as a child, to read minds, however, information I was receiving about their personal circumstances, was strictly from my dreams.

This was a sharp learning curve for me. It seemed that no matter how good, or honourable, intentions might be, it is important to respect the boundaries of others and only when invited, share intimate information and give advice.

CHAPTER SIX

Eat the Golden Apple and Share the Golden Rule

In the Bible we have references to communication from the dead to help the living.

And in Greece we have the Oracle at Delphi, where people sought help from those who had passed on.

It would seem that consulting the dead, or Spiritualism, is a universal practice and one which, through my dreams, I have found to be very valuable.

Contrary to assumptions by many people, it is not necessary to go to a Clairvoyant or Psychic, to connect to your dead relatives, to get whatever help you may be seeking, as we have many personal windows of opportunity to do so.

As stated earlier, around the anniversary of a death, or birthday of those in spirit, as well as around the anniversary of our own birthday, we have a six week period around the event, when the deceased move in closer around us, because we are thinking about them more frequently, at this time.

We can ask for any help we require and those in spirit will give a clue as to who the sender is.

After my father died, I used to have dreams in which I would receive a Franklin's bag of groceries every now and then.

My father, who was called Frank, was showing me that he was putting opportunities my way, represented by the bag of groceries.

The name of the local grocery store which was, Franklins, was used in the dream by my higher self, to indicate that the opportunities were from my father, who shared a similar name.

Unfortunately, when we experience grief at the death of a loved one, anger is often its companion, anger at being left behind, or anger because of feeling abandoned by the loved one, who has just died.

This anger, combined with the grief we feel, at the loss of the loved one, can create an impenetrable barrier around us and can often prevent the loved one from coming through in our dreams, to provide us, with dearly needed consolation.

Not only does this barrier prevent the deceased from making much desired contact, to console us, but it also prevents us from receiving other messages that they send, to help us in a more practical way.

I have found that meditation, or prayer, depending on one's personal belief system, helps enormously, to clear the channel of communication.

I have also found drawing to be of enormous help, to disperse anger.

To just draw without any particular image in mind, using coloured pencils or paints, will enable you, to get a better visual understanding, of your emotions and feelings and by bringing these feelings and emotions into your conscious mind, it you will be able to clear the situation more easily. (See section on colour symbolism).

It is only by becoming conscious of what the real problem in our lives is, at that particular point in time, which we can take appropriate action to deal with it.

When clients come to see me, and tell me that they are having difficulty connecting to those in spirit, or are having problems with a personal issue, I get the client to do a guided meditation, or visualization with me.

I find this to be a tremendous tool, to help unlock the unconscious mind and bring into consciousness, the real issue that is at the heart of their problem.

There is several good books in circulation, regarding this subject which can be purchased at book shops..

I have been told by my clients, that after seeing me and doing the visualization, they are able to access their dreams more easily.

An example of how important it is, to bring into consciousness, buried disappointments, or emotional hurts, is clearly demonstrated in the following encounter that I had with a client.

A vivacious, young Scottish woman, who came to see me for a reading, told me in the course of our conversation, that although she liked the idea of children, she was told by another Psychic, that because she suffered, from agonizing back pain, she would never have children.

Indeed, the young woman concerned, often had to spend long periods in hospital in traction, to help overcome the excruciating pain that she suffered.

I asked if she had also been advised by the medical profession, that she would be unlikely to have children, to which she replied in the negative.

I told the young woman, that the physical symptoms of back problems can sometimes be linked to emotional feelings, of being unsupported.

I asked the young woman, to think of a time when she had felt unsupported, at a significant point in her life, but she could not recall any such time.

I then suggested to the young woman, that she ask to be told in a dream, about any incident, that she may have forgotten about, that may be contributing to the problem.

I suggested, that once she brought the situation into consciousness, she would be able to solve the problem of her back pain, and thus enabling herself to get pregnant, if she so desired.

The young woman was horrified by my suggestion, and said that she didn't dream.

I informed her that we all dream, but we don't always remember our dreams. In fact, we have at least four or five dreams, each night and each dream is usually providing insight into a different aspect of the same situation. I told her that if she asked to remember her dreams, then she would do so.

However, the young woman told me that she would rather not do this, and asked if I would ask in a dream about the situation for her.

With her permission, to access her personal information, I agreed to the request.

That night, I had a dream, in which I saw the Irish nun, Breige Mc Kenna, who is renowned, in the Catholic Church, for her healing work and who tours the world, ministering to priests, who have suffered a crisis of faith.

Breige McKenna and I, were in a hotel room, and she appeared to be in a hurry and was packing a somewhat worn, but sturdy, brown suitcase, that was lying open on the bed.

In the dream, Breige McKenna paused for a moment, turned to me and said "the problem with your friend is that she fell out of a tree when she was eight".

Then she turned back to her suitcase and continued packing and I awakened from the dream.

When I related the dream to the young woman concerned, she said that she had never fallen out of a tree in her life.

I then explained the symbolism of the dream.

The tree represents the tree of life and opportunities available to us. To climb a tree in a dream indicates swift elevation in a chosen career.

To fall out of a tree, indicates that one has not been careful with their resources, and as a consequence lost out on success.

I suggested to the young woman that she could have suffered a disappointment, because she did not believe, that she would get the support that she needed for an opportunity that had come her way, and so had not only declined the opportunity, but had also regretted doing so.

The age of eight, related to the life path number eight, of my client, the number of those individuals, whose birth-right, under this auspicious vibration, is to be commercially successful, during this life-time. The disappointment could have related to a crucial career choice, that had not been given, the parental support, hoped for, resulting in an unsatisfactory, second choice of career, that did not offer, the same sense of personal satisfaction and fulfilment.

Also, as the young lady, was also born under the astrological sign of Aries, the sign of those who possess the least self-confidence in the zodiac, emotional support for major life decisions is crucial, to help encourage these individuals, to move forward in their lives.

As the first sign of the zodiac, these individuals possess a child-like trust, in the opinions of others, and often to their own detriment.

As soon as I explained the symbolism of the dream, the young woman exclaimed, "Oh my God, I know what it means, but I can't tell you".

Although I did feel a twinge of disappointment, at not being privy to my client's confidence, all that did matter was the birth of the young woman's son, the following year.

As for the psychic, who originally said that pregnancy would be out of the question for the young woman, her prediction was based on the young woman's attitude at the time, but we do however, need to be careful about the power of suggestion and creating a self- fulfilling prophecy.

However, the power of the mind is incredible, and by changing a belief system and our attitude, we can do, what may appear to be, the impossible.

In my dream the Irish nun, Breige McKenna represented me, and my desire to help the young woman.

Breige Mc Kenna, like me, was also born in Northern Ireland, and had also suffered from rheumatoid arthritis, and is also known to pass on messages, to those who come to her for a healing, from their loved ones, who are already in spirit.

The dream scenario of Breige McKenna, packing her suitcase, in the hotel room, corresponded to my personal circumstances of divorce, which was happening around that time, and the transitory nature of my situation.

As seen by this young woman's situation, the importance of clearing past hurts and disappointments cannot be emphasized enough. Sometimes, we bury them deep in our subconscious, where they can fester and poison any future opportunities for happiness.

Our souls are constantly sending messages to us in dreams, to alert us to situations which need to be dealt with.

The following dream is an example of this;

A twenty-five year old man, who was having emotional issues, in relating to his father, asked me to explain the following dream, which he had found unsettling.

In the dream, he had found himself in the house of his grandparents, where he had frequently stayed as a child.

It was night time in the dream, and he was lying in bed, as a young boy, and his younger brother, who shared the room with him had gone, as usual, into their father's room, because he had been frightened by a nightmare, a common occurrence for his younger brother.

In the dream, the young man himself was also frightened, and although his father was aware of this, didn't care about his fears as he favoured the younger brother.

The young man told me that in the dream, he was aware of a man, standing at the back door of the house, watching all that was going on, and although his father was aware of this, again, he didn't care.

Also in the dream, the young man could see a clock on the wall, which indicated that the time was 10 o' clock.

The time on the clock gives a clue to the message contained in the dream.

As the young man, is a life path ten in numerology, the dream was providing insight into his situation and what had been the cause of, his emotional distancing from his father.

The man in the dream, who was standing at the back of the house watching what was going on, is in fact a part of the young man's own personality. It is that part of the personality that, observes what happens around us, in a detached way, but records all that is going on in our subconscious, and when we are in a position to be able to deal with hurts and disappointments from childhood, this information will be brought into our consciousness, through the dreaming state, which provides a safe environment in which to deal with it.

Again, the importance of analysing dreams, to provide good health for the dreamer, is illustrated here.

The feelings of having been unfairly treated by his father, when he was a child, had coloured the young man's attitude to his father over the years, and so he was unable to share the same close relationship with his father, that his younger brother enjoyed.

The dreaming self does not judge, it simply observes situations and the information provided, allows us to understand why, we make the choices that we do, regarding our relationships.

It simply offers clarity to a situation that may be troubling us.

By addressing the situation that we are alerted to in our dreams, we may be liberated from the paralyzing inertia, of always having to appear to be "the good boy," or "the good girl," and so we are able to lead, more realistic and successful lives.

The soul is often referred to as a boat, or a ship, that has to navigate it's way through the emotional sea of life, where it faces constant danger of being dashed on the rocks of disappointment, or fails to detect a hidden reef of envy or jealousy, that lies in wait, to tear the hull apart with negative attitudes, of constant undermining and fault finding.

It is during these times, that messages in our dreams will provide us with the insight and courage necessary to stay on course.

Dreams that are frightening, especially of the nightmare kind, are usually alerting us to the immediate danger, of sabotaging ourselves, if we do not address a particular issue, or situation.

The term nightmare was originally used to refer to an evil spirit that visited people when they were asleep to seduce them and to gain complete possession of their soul or spirit."

The 'mare" or demon was called the, Incubus, and afflicted women, but was called the Succubus when it afflicted men.

Its presence in a dream left the dreamer feeling overpowered and oppressed.

One young woman, asked me to explain why she had nightmares, about something heavy, pressing on her chest and almost suffocating her.

I interpreted this dream, as that of the myth of the "Incubus" because of the young woman's lack of will power, in asserting herself regarding her career path, in the face of family opposition, and, becoming independent of them.

When I explained the myth to her, she agreed, that this was indeed the case and resolved the situation by following her dreams and is now a successful career woman without dreams of the Incubus.

Again this is an example of the cost to the individual that results from trying to please family members at the expense of the self.

Another young woman also had a similar experience.

Tearfully, the young woman told me of a recurring nightmare, which had plagued her over many years.

The nightmare had recurred again recently, but this time it had taken a slightly more sinister turn.

The usual form of the nightmare was that of an evil spirit, chasing her, but this time, the evil spirit was holding her feet in bed, preventing her from moving.

I immediately felt that she was being manipulated, into doing something that was not in her best interests.

I could see from her numerology chart, that her next life-change, indicated the need to follow her own individual, life-path, number of ten, which is enjoyment of life.

A severing of ties, either personally or professionally or both, was now necessary for her.

When the young woman made the appointment to see me, I had requested a dream from my higher self, to provide the information that the young woman needed to know.

In my dream, I had seen a beautifully appointed campervan, which had travelled through Germany and France, and then the campervan transformed into a minibus.

Just before the campervan transformed into the minibus, a tall, thin man, got out of the campervan, and I could see the lights of a town in the background.

The tall man then said," The lights in the town go on at 9 o' clock, in the evening, to keep them safe."

I said "I did not know that."

Then the minibus began to travel in a direction away, from the motorway.

I told the young woman, that the symbolism of the campervan, indicated enjoyment of life, by being independent and carefree, which as a life-path ten individual, was her birth-right.

The tall young man in the dream, represented her, as being a ten life-path individual, she was highly evolved spiritually, and was not inclined towards the pettiness, that lesser numbers may resort to, in getting their needs met.

Because the young man was thin, as well as tall, the symbolism suggested that she was not selfish in any way, nor was she receiving the emotional support that she deserved.

When one is plump in a dream, self-indulgence is indicated, just as slenderness, indicates lack of self-indulgence and possibly lack of support.

The minibus indicated a situation requiring group support in a small way, just as a larger bus, represents catering for community needs.

The tall man getting out of the campervan, just before it turned into a minibus, and the information, about protection for the people in the town, through the lights going on at 9 0' clock in the evening, suggests the life-path, change in direction, that occurs in the numerology chart every nine years, that would protect the young woman, from making decisions that would not be in her best interests.

The young woman told me that she loved to travel and had travelled extensively in the past, but, being the only daughter in a family of three, she felt under pressure to look after her parents, as they became older.

Clearly, from the life-path number, as well as indications on the birth chart and compounded with the nightmares that this young woman was having, she needed to follow her own star and not allow herself to be manipulated by guilt, (the evil spirit) into a lifetime of servitude.

I explained that certain life-path individuals, are happy to stay at home, and it is part of their life-time lessons to do so, but this was not the case for her and so the nightmares were sent by her soul, to force her to be true to herself.

The young woman felt very emotional at the realisation of how close she came, to denying herself the happiness in life which she was meant to have.

Not everyone, will experience a nightmare in this way, but in any nightmare, the underlying theme will be similar, regarding, asserting ones self, or resisting temptation..

CHAPTER SEVEN

Reincarnation and dreams.

To some, an allusion to reincarnation might be somewhat confronting, but the Irish have always believed in the transmigration of the soul, and in Ireland, paranormal activity and ghostly encounters are considered the norm.

The Irish accept that death walks hand and hand with life, and as warriors, were considered to be fearful in battle as they believed that the soul, which resided in the head, would pass from one body into another after death.

Two weeks before my father died, he had told my mother that if anything should suddenly happen to him, she was not to worry, as all his affairs were in order.

He had also said something similar to me, on the morning that I had set off, for Australia, telling me that if he should die before I returned, not to worry, as he had made his peace with God.

My father did not fear death as he did not see death as the end, but rather a stage of transition from one life to the next.

It is quite ironic, that the symbolism of dancing in a dream can indicate that we are in touch with the rhythms of life, as my father did in actual fact die, while he was dancing with my aunt at the wedding of one of my brothers.

He had a massive heart attack, and was unable to be revived.

Everyone who was present agreed, after the initial shock, that my father did indeed; get the happy death, he had always prayed for.

My grandmother had a similar attitude to death, and a year before she died, had shown me the "Glory Box" at the end of her bed, where she kept the garments in which she wanted to be buried.

I believe that we all have a sense of our own mortality, and like my father, who may appear to die so suddenly, have a sense of what is about to happen, and so put their house in order.

Connecting to those who are already on the other side, through the dreaming state, will not cause you to begin having ghostly visitations.

The dead are not trying to frighten anyone, they simply want to help.

What I have discovered from contacting my relatives who have passed into the spirit world, is that help will only be given, if it is in our best interests, as can be seen from the following dream.

Like many of the Irish people, my father had a keen interest in horses and one of his passions, was buying and selling retired race- horses.

I decided, that I would call on his help, to place a winning bet on the Australian Melbourne Cup, to test my theory, of the dead looking after the living.

But first, I decided to ask for his help at a lesser venue, to be sure that he was going to help me.

And so, I asked my father to tell me in a dream, the name of a horse that would win a particular race, on a specified day.

That night I had a dream in which someone said to me," I'm sorry, it's ten, ten, ten, and ten". Four tens, I thought. So ignoring the apology before hand, I placed a bet, on horse number ten, race four.

When the horse came second, I understood the significance of the apology.

My father was letting me know that, yes, the dead do look after the living, but he was not going to encourage me to gamble, instead, I would have to work hard, and earn my own money.

So whether we like it or not, those in spirit will often save us from our own bad habits.

I have also discovered that the dead continue their journey on the other side of the veil, and as subsequent family members die, they take over the responsibility of helping the living, while those who have gone before them continue to evolve on the other side. I was made privy to this information one night when three decades after my father died, I requested his help, but received the following message in my dream.

"Do not disturb your father, he is asleep upstairs.'

When someone is asleep in a dream, it means that they are unavailable to the dreamer at that point in time.

The fact that my father was upstairs, in the dream, indicated that he had progressed on his spiritual journey, and now was on a different spiritual plain and no longer available to help me.

The thought did cross my mind however, that my father might have reincarnated on the earth plain and that was the reason for his unavailability.

How many times have we looked into the eyes of a new born baby only to remark, "this is an old soul", because of the wisdom that we see there, and then a few weeks later, when we look again, we see only blankness?

It is as if, when the baby is born into this world, for one brief moment, it retains knowledge of previous experiences, but, as it becomes acclimatized to its new, earthly surroundings, the knowledge fades into the background.

However, we are often amazed, at the little gems of wisdom, which young children possess.

My three year old niece announced to her father one morning, that next time, she would be his mother, and that he would have more hair, causing great astonishment amongst family members.

The early Christian Church believed in reincarnation and the impact it had on the present life as well as consequences for future reincarnations.

However as a matter of expediency for the early Christian Church, and to cultivate the favour and protection of the emperor, at the time, reincarnation was declared to be a heretical doctrine, and those who believed in it thereafter, were put to death.

We might not suffer the same punishment today, but as our belief system provides us with a sense of security, as well as, a sentimental connection to our family and cultures and any new ideas, are viewed with suspicion and distrust, even an old belief, which is made new again.

I would suggest that when asking for help in a dream of family members, who have passed on, be mindful of the passing of time.

Other Blocks in Dreams

A gentleman, whom I met and whose father was in spirit, had a gambling addiction which had contributed to the disintegration of his marriage.

When I met him, he was recovering from a double knee operation, and was feeling very sorry for himself. He asked me to explain a dream that had been troubling him.

In his dream, he saw himself living in a cardboard box on the street.

I did not know at this point that he had a gambling addiction, but explained that whatever he was doing at the moment was going to lead him into a state, of financial destitution.

It was then that he disclosed his gambling addiction.

The man had already gambled away, fifty thousand dollars that year, so his father who was in Spirit, was, I believe, showing him the direction in which he was heading.

Needless to say, it was a sobering and timely warning, and the gentleman took the necessary steps to prevent the warning in the dream, from becoming a reality.

I believe the man's addiction was in part, the consequence of unresolved grief at the death of his father, when he was twelve years old.

He had told me previously, that no one had taken the time to talk to him about his father's death, as every one was preoccupied with their own grief, and he had felt alone in his grief, and had difficulty coming to terms with the impact, of the sudden death.

He had also told me of another dream that he had, before the dream of destitution, which led me to believe that that two situations were linked together.

In his dream, moss was growing on the ceiling of his house, and he had felt a sense of disquiet about the dream.

I explained to him, that the ceiling in his dream represented the way he thought about his father's death and his inability to deal with his grief.

Moss, which usually grows where there is inadequate water drainage, was symbolic of the grief, he had felt at his father's death, that had congealed in his mind and was unable to drain away naturally, because of insufficient emotional support, from those around him, and was most likely impacting, on his ability to deal with the rigors of life.

The fact that his father had died, before the onset of his teenage years, may have contributed to a failure, to successfully navigate the rite of passage through puberty and into manhood, because of the lack of strong male role model. This could have contributed to the man's lack of self discipline and perhaps, to his gambling habit.

Without the guidance of a positive father image, guiding him into manhood and the responsibilities expected of him, a young man may become like a ship without a rudder that is tossed about in the sea, of unchecked emotions and self indulgence.

The importance of a strong role model, in the life of a young man, is beautifully explored through the medium of the, Grimm brother's fairytale, of "Iron John" by Robert Bly and is recommended reading.

For many of us, the soul may get stuck at certain events in our lives, which were too traumatic at the time, for the soul to deal with and perhaps, we, did not get the help necessary, to cope with the situation.

As a consequence, the soul may get stuck at that particular point and has difficulty moving on and as a consequence, opportunities in life may have been missed, or, were unable to be taken.

To rescue the soul, takes time, we need to go back to the particular event, that is affecting the progress of the soul, and have the courage to face, whatever lies behind the closed door. We need to understand the impact it has had, on the life of the soul, and set about repairing the damage.

Our nightmares often serve this purpose, they force us to address the potential consequences of unresolved issues, and therefore learning to understand our dreams will lead us towards emotional and psychological good health.

The following dream, is a clear example of the impact unresolved issues, may have on an individual's life path.

A middle aged lady, who suffered greatly from low self esteem, confided in me, that she constantly felt anxious about situations and avoided being the centre of attention. The client also said that despite having achieved good academic qualifications, avoided opportunities, to improve her financial status, as it would mean being thrust into the lime light, a position that she constantly avoided.

I decided, that perhaps a different approach was needed to this situation and so decided to use my skill in palmistry, to unlock the root cause of this lady's problem, as the hand is a reflection of our thoughts and emotions.

I had developed an interest in palmistry years earlier in my teaching career, when I had been approached, by the middle management, of a Catholic High School where I was teaching at the time, to give assistance to a year eleven student, who wished to investigate psychic phenomena, as a study, for her Higher School Certificate.

To help this student, I had offered, with the permission of the student's family and the good will of the school, to accompany the student to a palmistry workshop that I knew was being held in Sydney, that week-end, to enable her to learn first hand, about this discipline, and enable the student, to document her findings for her Higher School Certificate project.

As a result of this undertaking, I developed an interest in palmistry myself and have continued to study it over the years. I have been amazed at the insight that palmistry can provide, about the characteristics, as well as, personality traits, and other information, peculiar to certain individuals.

I discovered, after a few moments of examination of my client's hand, that the line of the heart, in both palms, indicated a negative impact on her life, through unresolved issues from childhood, and that, these issues were still affecting the way that she viewed her opportunities in life.

In fact, the direction of the lines across the palm, suggested that she may have experienced abuse as a child.

I explained what the lines of her palms suggested and advised her that childhood abuse takes many forms. I suggested that she use her dreams to discover the type of abuse that may have affected her, as whatever happened, was still impinging on her enjoyment of life.

Initially the lady vehemently rejected this information, but returned to see me later and told me, that her mother's off' handed response, to her suggestion that she was abused as a child of, "That doesn't surprise me", confirmed in her mind, the accuracy of what I had suggested and the client also felt that, her mother's reaction, also suggested that the abuse may have been sexual abuse.

When the lady returned a third time to see me, she told me, that she had asked to be told in a dream, if she had been abused when she was a child, and she shared the following dreams with me.

She had a dream of a door, behind which she knew, there was a yellow snake.

She was told in the dream to open the door, and that if she did so, she would get a healing.

And then, she woke up out of her sleep.

The next night, she asked to be shown what lay behind the door, and had a dream, in which she was standing outside the backdoor of the family home, where she had grown up.

In the dream, she was a little child, about the age of three.

As she went to go to the back door, her heart began to pound and she felt terrified, and fled, without going through the door, and suddenly woke up.

As the lady was now determined to find out what lay behind the door, she asked, before going to sleep the following night, to be given the courage to face, whatever was behind the door.

That night in her dream, she was aware of a very tall and very beautiful lady, who wearing a wide, brimmed hat, and was standing outside the back door of her family home.

A voice said to her, "Go with Jane, you will be safe with her"

The beautiful lady then took her by the hand, and together they went towards the back door of the house.

Finally, she managed to go through the back door of the house, and she found herself at the bottom of a staircase, which was only dimly lit.

She began to climb up the stairs (which represented making progress in her life), and as she did so, her father suddenly stepped out of the shadows, but as a younger man, and she woke up.

The importance of the symbolism of, the back door, of the family home, in the dream, represented the opportunity of going back to the past, to re-visit family issues.

The lady told me, that the information in the dream helped her to understand so many things about her life.

She said, that she had often felt guilty as she was growing up, because her father appeared to be more generous towards her, than to her brothers and sisters and she realised now, that he was feeling guilty about what had happened, and was trying to compensate in some way.

The lady said, that the information given in the dreams, had also helped to explain why she had felt so ugly when growing up, and why in later years, when she had found photos of herself, the faces, in the different photographs, had been blacked out. The lady said, that she then remembered, that she had blackened the faces in the photographs herself, as at the time, she had thought, that she had looked ugly compared to her brothers and sisters.

Also, the habit that she had, of constantly washing her hands, because they always felt dirty, and her obsession with cleanliness as a young girl, which made her the butt of family humour, could now be understood.

The lack of drive in her career, because of a reluctance to be in the limelight due to low self esteem, could now, also, be explained.

The client, also discovered from her mother, that her father had an Aunt Jane, who had died many years before, and who had been a nun, and who was known, as a very kind- hearted individual, who went out of her way to help others.

The ancient Greeks were known to have built shrines, to serve as healing centres, in which people who needed a healing would be placed.

During the night, Aesculapius the god of healing, would come down in the form of a yellow snake, and heal them.

As yellow symbolizes the intellect, and a door represents an opportunity, I knew that the lady was being given an opportunity, to change the way she thought and felt about a situation from her past, and all she had to do was to take it.

As a snake, is able to shed its skin, so this lady would now, be able to shed the skin of the past, and create a new and more positive life, for herself. It is also interesting to note, that the lady, herself, was born in the Chinese year of the snake, an auspicious sign in itself.

The beautiful lady in the dream represented an aspect of the dreamer's own personality, that she was not yet aware of, and the symbol of the wide brimmed hat, represented protection for the way she was thinking about the situation, as anything to do with the head, is usually pointing to the mind and thoughts of the dreamer.

Any unknown person in a dream can represent an aspect of the dreamer's own personality, which has not yet come into consciousness, and can indicate the need, to take a fresh look at a situation.

The setting of the dream was able to throw light on the time of life that the emotional energies were repressed, because of an inability to deal with them at that time.

We often learn from each other, and the student can often become the teacher.

The courage of my client to address the issues from her past encouraged me to also revisit issues from childhood, where sibling rivalry can leave its mark in our formative years.

And so shortly after this encounter, when I had occasion to return to Ireland, I stopped off en route, in Glastonbury and did a re-birthing course, which, although confronting at the time, helped me to let go, of a great deal of my past hurts, caused by being too sensitive as a child.

The re-birthing course came about, because of a dream that I had, the night before the visit to Glastonbury.

I had been staying with my youngest brother, Fergus in London, and it was he who had suggested going to visit Stonehenge and Glastonbury, as I had a delay, with my flight- connection, to Ireland.

The dream was simple and very brief. In the dream, I saw a little snow leopard, coming out of a pool of water.

I could not understand the significance at first, but when I visited a Healing Centre in Glastonbury the following day, I marvelled at finding a picture, of the exact scene from my dream, in a book that I had picked up to leaf through, entitled," The Golden Cauldron" by Nicki Scully, and I felt that serendipity was at play here.

In her book, Nicki Scully, uses the symbolism of a snow leopard, to confront fear and the picture from the book, was the exact image that appeared in my dream, the night before.

I knew at once, that I was meant to be at this Healing Centre and that I was going to get help in some way.

I checked out the workshops offered, and decided to do a residential, meditation course, which involved a, five-day residence, on the premises.

During one of the mealtime gatherings, I struck up a conversation with a girl who was doing a re-birthing workshop.

When the girl described what was involved in the re-birthing workshop, a requirement getting into a hot-tub naked, with the male facilitator, and doing a particular breathing exercise, I decided that it would be too confronting for me. Also, I was somewhat suspicious, of the necessity of being naked, but I said that I applauded her courage, for doing so.

That night however, I had a dream, in which I was shown a long road, and someone in the dream said "The Eye of Horus is a lonely road".

And I had indeed, received a vision of "The Eye of Horus" many years previously, after a meditation, failing at the time, to understand its significance.

According to the beliefs set out in the Egyptian, "Book of the Dead", Horus was a type of Messiah, who was reborn every 2500 years, in his journey to perfectionism.

As I am on the life-path number seven, which is the number of the transformer, the one who will change Karmic patterns in their family of origin, I was being given insight into how lonely this life-path can be and the desirability of having a companion.

I knew that the dream was referring to my Catholic upbringing, and its indoctrination, regarding sex and the physical body, and the shame associated with the naked body. Although, no longer a practicing Catholic, the remnants of my puritanical upbringing, still occasionally, crept in unnoticed, and manifested at unexpected times, in a slightly, prudish outlook towards sex, that needed to be addressed.

My dreams seemed to indicate, that despite being divorced, it was in my best interests to have a partner, to share my life path.

And so the next day, despite my reservations, I booked in and paid for the workshop, before I had the chance to get cold feet and change my mind.

As well as addressing psychological and emotional issues, the dreaming state can also give us information about our past lives, as difficult situations that we are confronted with in the present, can represent karmic issues, or challenges, that we may not have dealt with adequately, in previous lifetimes, and the present situation provides an opportunity, to make a better judgment.

One such opportunity presented itself, while I was working in an organization, where bullying and harassment were common practice. I had decided to take a stand against such behaviour and during a very testing period, I had a dream that I was in the catacombs in Rome. In the dream, I picked up pieces of gold, from the floor of the cave, and speaking in Italian, a language that I have never studied, but understood in my dream, I said,

"My name is Peter and this is my gold!"

I believe that in a previous life times, I may have been persecuted for my beliefs and needed to take a stand, and perhaps did not have the courage to do so, which is why, in this lifetime, I have been born under the astrological sign of, Aries.

This star sign, is influenced by the red planet Mars, and is associated with aggressive energy, vigour and courage, as well as Ares, the Greek God of war, who loves combat and the clash of arms. Also, being a seven life-path in numerology, I have the internal fortitude necessary, to do battle for my beliefs, which provides much needed support for the cross, that I have clearly defined on the palm of my left hand, indicating that this life-time, I will constantly encounter opposition.

Indeed, at the time, I needed all the fortitude that I could muster. Having no legal representation and no legal experience, I was dependant, on the information that I received in my dreams each night, to navigate my way, through the Australian Court system, despite underhanded tactics, that those in powerful positions often resort to.

When analyzing dreams, it is useful to pay attention to the themes, running through dreams, as they are alerting the dreamer to life time lessons, that need to be addressed, in each reincarnation.

Also, an awareness of the astrological sign which one is born under provides a clue, to the lessons needed, for personal growth, as well as personal strengths at the dreamer's disposal.

Dreams prepare us for change, and more especially so, through our nightmares.

I often tell people, that a nightmare is our best friend, as it is warning us, that there is a situation around us in the present, that we need the courage to change, or we will sabotage ourselves.

Again the dreaming mind, will shed light on this situation, if we have the courage to ask.

One lady, who came to have a reading, was having relationship difficulties with her partner.

Prior to the Reading, she had asked to be given information that she needed to know in a dream, and now wanted clarification, about what she was shown in the dream.

In the dream, she saw a girl, try to push a young man into a swimming pool.

As the girl did so, she could see the look of horror on the young mans his face, but he managed to keep his balance.

The swimming pool represents the committed or structured relationship that the lady wanted to have with her partner, but his look of horror, indicated quite clearly that he did not reciprocate her feelings, about a commitment to the relationship.

It was time for the lady concerned to look else where for a relationship.

However being born under the sign of Taurus the bull, this lady was very stubborn and territorial, an unfortunate, negative aspect, of this good natured, star sign and so she was having trouble accepting that the relationship, was not going to develop into something more permanent.

Again, the astrological star sign gives a clue, to lessons needing to be learned in this lifetime, and unfortunately, the messages we receive in our dreams can be brutally honest.

I too, discovered this when I moved into a house-share, with a work colleague.

Initially, we got on famously together, and even her boyfriend seemed to enjoy the extra company.

Then I began to feel that all was not well, and I asked to be told in a dream, if I should move.

In my dream, someone said, quite indifferently,

"Why stay where you are not wanted?"

I moved out the next day.

CHAPTER EIGHT

Consolation from the Dead

When a loved one dies, those left behind, sometimes seek proof of the afterlife for reassurance that they will eventually, be reunited with their loved ones.

The death of a child is particularly hard to bear, and the years that pass, are often a constant source of grief for what might have been, and now, never will be.

Yet these children, who are now in spirit, constantly watch over those who are left behind and try to connect with them, a fact that I discovered, after I acquired a new dancing partner.

After I met my dancing partner, Roy, I had a dream in which I saw liquorice allsorts "lollies," and I had a flash of a monkey, and someone in the dream said, "He will enjoy these!".

When I awoke the next morning, I could not make, head nor tail, of the message. However, when my friend Roy and I, went to a local market the next day, on one of the stalls, I saw three little terracotta monkeys, in liquorice allsorts colours and so I bought them and gave them to Roy, telling him, that I had a dream, informing me that he would enjoy them.

Not surprisingly, Roy didn't know what to make of me, or the terracotta monkeys.

Then a truly surprising thing happened. When Roy turned one of the monkeys upside down to examine it, on the base of the monkey, Roy discovered that the name, Olivia, had been etched; it was the name of his baby daughter who had died at three months of age.

Both Roy and I were amazed, as his daughter Olivia, had obviously been the person contacting me in my dream, the night before.

Now, when I meet other people, who have similar situations of family loss, I tell them about this connection, in the hope that it will give them some consolation, to know that they are being constantly looked after, by their loved one in spirit.

Also, baby Olivia would now be a young lady of nineteen had she lived. I believe that after a child dies, they continue to age, in accordance with the age of the living child, that they would have been, unless, or until, they reincarnate.

Interestingly enough, just after this incident, Roy had a dream in which he found a silver box, which was filled with treasure.

In the dream he was really excited, as he knew that the treasure was extremely valuable and woke up feeling very happy.

The next day, Roy and I were browsing around a collectable shop, when to his great surprise Roy found the silver box, from his dreams.

With great anticipation, he opened the box, but was disappointed to discover, not the valuable treasure that he expected find, but a Bible, lying inside.

I tried, unconvincingly, to console Roy, by explaining that the treasure in the dream was in fact the treasure within himself, which he had discovered, or unearthed, by tapping into his spirituality through his dreams. A treasure that is priceless!

When my mother-in-law died, my older son was inconsolable, as the bond between him and his grandmother was very close, and he missed her dreadfully.

Then, he had a dream about her, which helped him come to terms with the loss, and move on with his life.

In his dream, he climbed up a ladder, which was leaning against a wall.

When he got to the top of the ladder, his grandmother was there, but there was a divide between where she was, and where he was standing on the ladder.

She told him, that he would not like where she was, and to go back down the ladder.

The divide in the dream indicates the divide, between the living and the dead.

The ladder in the dream indicates the spiritual effort needed to connect with those in spirit. The wall indicates either a barrier, or support depending on the context of the dream.

His grandmother's warning to him, would seem to indicate that his grandmother was telling him, that she was aware of how deeply saddened he was, by her death and even though he missed her enormously, it was not yet time, for him to join her.

After this dream, he still thought about his grandmother, but the sense of loss had left him, as he knew she was around him, watching over him.

Sometimes a light suddenly going out in a dream, may indicate a death, but the light being deliberately switched off, has a different meaning, and indicates the death of a relationship, as you know it, but not the death of the person.

Just before my divorce, I had a dream, in which I saw my then husband, in a room, sitting, at a table writing. As I watched him in the dream, he got up, switched off the light, and went out of the room, closing the door behind him.

I felt a profound sense of loss, and sadness when I woke up.

Writing in a dream, represents communication.

The room represents an opportunity, or an aspect of one's life, and the action of the light being switched off, indicates the deliberate action, of terminating a situation.

The closing of the door represented the finality of the decision.

After I became divorced, I wanted reassurance that I would be protected, by Divine Energy, and I wanted to know, how I would be aware of this help.

I had a dream, in which, I was in a crypt, where sarcophagi lined the walls. As I went past each sarcophagus, an eye on top of each sarcophagus, opened up, and looked at me and finally as I reached the end of the crypt, I could see the big brown eye, of a large, dark horse that was standing at the door, looking at me.

As my father was born in the Chinese year of the Horse, I knew then, that he and the dead were looking out for me.

Divorce is usually the last resort to a situation, which we no longer find tenable.

However, not everyone can cope with the emotional upheaval, such a decision brings, and when a close friend confided in me, that she felt she should get a divorce from her partner, as she was very unhappy, I suggested that she check out in her dream, if it was in her best interest, to do so, and advised her to use the simple technique mentioned earlier.

When she rang me the next day, my friend said that she would not be getting a divorce after all.

In her dream, she said that, she and I had been in a small room together, where there was a little window.

My friend had watched in the dream, as I had crawled through this little window, and just as she was about to follow me, she said, "I don't want to do this", and she woke up.

The room represented the situation we were both in, and the little window represented one small window of opportunity, that we both had, at that particular time, to change a situation.

Again, cultural backgrounds and belief systems have a huge impact on our ability to move forward in our lives.

My friend, who is under the astrological sign of Virgo, the home- maker, as well as being on the life path of the number four which signifies, patience and hard work, and because my friend's personal experience of childhood, had not been a happy one, her desire not to subject her own son to a similar fate, had I believe, greatly influenced her unconscious decision.

Also, as both parents of my close friend are in spirit, I can not rule out the possibility, that they too, influenced her decision.

Family members, who are in spirit, will often give information, on an intimate level, to identify who they are, and this immediately establishes the connection.

When my mother was alive, she often used to tell us, that she was a year younger than the Queen of England.

Just after she died, she turned up in my dream, and looked just like the Queen, to reassure me that she was watching over me.

When my older son was looking for part-time bar work, he was one of several applicants, at a local club, where only one position, was available.

I asked to be told in a dream, if he would be successful.

I was told in a dream that, "the Clydesdale horses are the biggest horses and pull the brewery carts."

I knew then, that he would get the job, as his grandfather, who is now in spirit, had been called Clyde, and the word Clydesdale, had been a play on words, which often happens in a dream, and it was also, two weeks before the anniversary of his grandfather's birthday.

Interestingly enough, when we see the dead unexpectedly in a dream, it is not a good sign for the dreamer, as it is a warning dream.

In that particular case, the dreamer is being alerted to a past situation, which may be impacting on the present, and not in the dreamer's best interests.

Usually, the dream will relate to people, or situations from the past, which were not adequately dealt with at the time, and similar situations are now occurring in the present.

CHAPTER NINE

Health; Remedies and Advice

When I became ill, I read as many books, on natural therapies, as possible.

I began using a cold pressed, peanut oil massage, once a week and was amazed at how much it relieved the pain of arthritis.

I had read about its benefits, in a book, written about the life, of Edgar Cayce, who had been, a renowned healer, in North America, when he was alive.

In fact the masseur, whom I engaged, to give me a massage, once a week, was so impressed by the results, that he began recommending its use, to all his other clients, who did not have any peanut allergies.

I found this ironic, as he had raised his eyebrows in surprise, when I had initially turned up at his clinic, with my bottle of cold, pressed, peanut oil.

Much later, after I had, with the help of the Peanut oil rub, lost the stiffness and much of the pain in my joints, I had a dream telling me, that if I ate ginger every day, I would have good health for the rest of my life.

As ginger increases the circulation of blood to the heart, this in turn benefits the skin and all the other organs of the body, and I have found, that not only are my joints in much better condition, but, I also, no longer suffer from, Raynauds disease. It is a painful condition, often common to women, who have an under-active thyroid gland. The condition, causes the fingers, to swell and throb and become first pale, then blue and then red. The condition is often precipitated, by either feeling cold, or by emotional distress.

From the information that I have received over the years, regarding my own health, as well as, recommendations for the health of other people, I believe that once we make the commitment for good health, we will get all the help that we need, in our dreams, whether it is solicited or not, as I discovered after my divorce.

I had become a bit of a recluse after my divorce, because of my sensitivity to the negative opinions of others, as well as censure that I incurred from family members, and I spent most of my time, reading whatever material I could find, regarding health matters and spirituality.

I have read that there is an unspoken belief amongst doctors, that if a person has a chronic illness, they will be much healthier than everyone else, as they will take better care of their health.

I must admit, that I have found some truth in this, and it was confirmed in a dream that I had, where I saw myself gathering herbs and I was told in the dream, that I was the healthiest in my family, as drinking herbal tea had become a way of life for me.

From a conversation with my mother, after his death, I discovered, that my father had also, been a believer, in the efficacy of herbal tea for good health. My mother told me, that she used to gather fresh dandelions every spring, to make dandelion herbal tea for my father.

She also told me, that my father had an aunt, who was born with a caul over her head, which is the mark of a Healer. Not only did my great aunt, use her gift, to help the family, but, she was also in much demand, in the local community.

However, being so reclusive was not so good for my psychological health, and I was shown in a dream, that my "Happy" plant, was dying from lack of water. In my dream, I was told to do what I'd always done, and to "go dancing".

I did in actual fact have a large "Happy" plant that had been a present, many years earlier, from my younger brother Chris, which he had won as, "Salesman of the Month". However as the "Happy" plant was thriving, I knew that it was not the subject of the dream. I knew that the dream was referring to my need for more enjoyment of life.

When analysing a dream, it is important to consider any associations, or connections, between the symbols, places, events, images and people in the dream, to your conscious life experiences.

Dreams provide us with insight, as well as self-discovery, and the details in the dream, colours, shapes, smells, and people who are present in the dream, can provide a clue to the period, or circumstance, of your life that the dream is referring to.

And so, I decided that I would go dancing, and learn to rock n' roll.

Needless to say, there were enormous, psychological and physical benefits to learning a style of dancing, as well as, the social interaction needed, for my personal "Happy" plant.

I had in fact spent my formative years learning Irish Dancing, and when I was studying to teach High School, I had trained as an English teacher with a subsidiary subject of Modern Dance, so dancing was something that I thoroughly enjoyed, as well as being familiar with.

Another interesting aspect of dreams is the help given, to find the origin of a health condition.

As a young boy, my older son used to suffer the debilitating effects of severe migraine headaches, which were causing him great distress.

I asked for a dream to show me the underlying cause, of the migraine headaches.

In my dream, I saw the birth canal and my son, as a baby in the birth canal, and a pair of forceps suddenly inserted, grasping my son's head and pulling him out.

My son had indeed been a forceps delivery, as well as having been induced, and the overlapping bones due to the use of forceps, had according to the attending gynaecologist, given my son a headache.

I explained to my son, that as he had not been ready of his own accord, to traverse the birth canal, instead being forced into the situation and then being painfully wrenched from the birth canal, he now remembered that painful episode, each time he felt forced into a situation, that he did not feel prepared for and so gave himself a migraine.

To counter these feelings of insecurity, I suggested that in future, he ask for information in his dreams, regarding any situations that he felt might cause him worry and distress, and this he agreed to do.

My son no longer suffers from migraine, and he continues to seek whatever help he needs from his dreams, as can be seen from dreams in his teenage years, when he suffered the usual teenage problems of acne, and no matter what treatment he used, nothing seemed to clear up the pimples on his face.

He asked me for ideas, as medication didn't seem to work and I told him to ask in his dreams what was causing the pimples, and then he would be able to get rid of them.

The following morning, he announced that the peanut butter sandwiches, that I was giving him for school lunch, were causing the problem.

He said that he had a dream, in which a friend of his was looking in a mirror, and as his friend did so he said, "Peanut butter sandwiches are giving me pimples."

My son knew that he was a reflection of his friend, in that they were both in the same year, at the same school and both astrological Air signs. Also, he and his friend had pimples.

Of course I stopped giving my son peanut butter sandwiches, and the pimples cleared up. Obviously my son, who has oily skin naturally, could not tolerate the extra oil of the peanuts.

Years later, when my son began to get pimples again, I told him to ask once more for information about the cause of the pimples, in his dreams.

The next day he told me that the Beer he was drinking was causing the pimples.

He then said, "I will just stick with the beer!"

As the saying goes,

"You can lead a horse to water, but you cannot make it drink."

I learned from this little incident, that not everyone will take the advice offered in their dreams.

When I asked to be given a solution for a friend who suffered the embarrassment of too much wind, I was given the answer in the following way.

In the dream, I found myself in a convenience shop, where a lady was serving behind the counter.

I went up to the lady and said "I would like something for wind."

The lady simply said, "You need to drink soda water."

When I told my friend this, he was amazed and said that the response explained something, which used to puzzle him years earlier.

When he was a sailor, and he and his friends would go on a boozy night out, one of his companions would also drink soda water during the evening.

The next morning, all the sailors from the previous evening, except the one who had been drinking the soda water, suffered dreadfully, from severe bouts of flatulence, and he could not until now, understand why.

It is not only for people, that we are given advice in dreams, but attention to nature is also addressed.

Many years ago, I had bought a beautiful plant, to put in my brightly lit bathroom, but after a few months, I decided to put it in the living-room, to brighten up a dull corner.

The night after I did this, I had a dream in which someone said, "The plant doesn't like it in the living-room, put it back where it was".

Surprised and somewhat amused, I thought, "now the plants are talking to me as well", but I returned the plant to the bathroom, and shortly after the plant put forth several new shoots.

A few years after this, I bought an expensive Bonsai tree, which resembled a little man with bulging muscles. I placed it in my older son's bedroom, as his father was a keen body builder and I thought my son would get pleasure from looking at the little Bonsai tree. It happily resided in my son's bedroom for several months, until one night, when I had a dream, warning me, that it was giving off toxic air.

When I examined the plant, I discovered that the little tree had collapsed internally, and was no longer healthy, so that evening I placed it outside on the lawn, but the next morning it was gone.

Hopefully, whoever recycled the little Bonsai tree, did not suffer any adverse effects from it.

On a more serious note, we can all get help if we just ask, but so few people realize this.

A work colleague of mine confided in me, that the breast cancer that she thought she had recovered from had returned and so she was going to retire from work. Being a great believer in the efficacy of herbal tea, I suggested that she ask to be told in a dream, the name of an herbal tea, which might be of help to her and her condition.

My colleague was surprised when I told her to do this, as although she did often get information in her dreams, she hadn't known that you could ask a specific question, and so she agreed to do this.

The next day at work, she searched me out to tell me, that in her dream, she was told to drink Hibiscus tea, as it has the highest antioxidants. Now I advise everyone to drink this tea that may have cancer, of any type.

A female condition of, Endometrioses, was brought to the attention of one client, when she had a dream in which she was shown, that her sitting room was old and dark, and dilapidated, with wallpaper, peeling off the walls.

As the sitting-room of the house, is the social hub of the home, and if we consider the house as representing the body, then the most sociable aspect of the body is the womb.

Wallpaper often lines the walls of a sitting-room, just as Endometriosis can line the walls of the female womb, which had happened to this lady, and was confirmed by her Gynaecologist.

A male client, who had been a builder all his life, suffered from severe pain in his hips and although retired for several years, likened the pain, to the pressure of the heavy tool/nail bag, which used to be strapped around his waist.

Using the simple dream technique, he asked for advice and was told to drink lime juice, which, although seemed to be an almost, unbelievably simple, solution to his painful condition, cured the problem within three days.

Happily years later, the client still remains free, from that painful condition.

Often, we are too busy getting on with life, to notice little changes in our health, which if not dealt with immediately, will have long term consequences.

When I was forty-three, I had a dream in which my older son again, appeared.

In the dream my son said, "Mum, I need hormone replacement therapy, to keep my testicles healthy and to keep me young looking".

I woke up thinking "Oh my God, I'm in the menopause!"

I made an appointment with my Gynaecologist, and sure enough, I had just started menopause.

My son's testicles symbolized my ovaries, and the need to use hormone treatment to keep them healthy and to look younger, referred to the aging acceleration, because of a lack of oestrogen, which happens after menopause.

As we are all individuals, we do not necessarily tolerate the same types of medication and there was a great deal of controversy around taking hormone-replacement therapy at the time, but I had no doubt that it was necessary for my health to take it, as I had absolute faith in the information, given to me in my dreams.

In another dream that I had, I saw a frying pan in which bacon and eggs were being cooked. A voice said to me,

"You are eating yourself to death."

I got such a shock, as I am of a slim build, and I do not as a rule, eat bacon and eggs, fried in a frying pan.

However, I had been eating a boiled egg for breakfast every morning that week, and I had been having ham sandwiches, for lunch, hence the dream of bacon and eggs.

My father had died at the age of sixty-four, from a massive heart attack, brought about by hardened arteries, and from the dream, it would seem that I had a predisposition to heart problems.

I did have a cholesterol test after that, and discovered that I had an unexpectedly high cholesterol count, which I managed to bring quickly under control, by cutting eggs and ham out of my diet, which surprised my doctor.

CHAPTER TEN

Numerology in Dreams

As mentioned previously, each life-path number has a particular influence on our lives, often known as a vibration, according to the philosophical belief of, Numerology.

If we understand how this vibration applies to each of us as individuals, we can understand why, we sometimes appear to be at loggerheads with our loved ones, while with others, even complete strangers, we have a complete harmony of purpose.

Numerology in our dreams, can indicate the vibration we need, to learn our lessons from, on our life path, and how our connection to certain individuals and situations, facilitate these lessons for us.

It is only through friction, that movement is possible, and it is usually from those people who cause us the most friction, that we learn our most valuable lessons.

We do need to keep in mind that, one particular number is not better than another; it is the life-path, which a person is experiencing, during a particular lifetime.

The following, is a brief synopsis, of the influence of particular numbers, on our life-path and the meaning that they may hold in our dreams.

One; The number of, Ego, completion, sociable, courageous, creative, controlling, organized, selfish, intuitive, balanced, letting go.

Two; The number of, Duality, wisdom, relationship guru, modest, diplomatic, clever, nurturing, needy, manipulative.

Three; The number of Extravert, communicator, actor, chameleon, business acumen, critical, talented, social climber, opportunities.

Four; The Number of Artistic, dependable, perfectionist, workaholic, worrier, helpful, materialistic, controlling, critical, organized, patient, jealous, foundation.

Five; The number of, Clever, independent, commitment-phobic, emotionally intense, knowledgeable, controlling, brilliant, non-communicative, spiteful. The five senses, arguments, movement, change.

Six; The number of, Home, family loyalty, nurturing, creative, feminine, private, modest, lacking perseverance and ambition, materialistic, charming, anxious, motherly, career opportunities, children.

Seven; The number of, Teacher, psychic, priest/priestess, God's number, trusting, naive, dreamer, idealist, sensitive, creative, versatile, highly-strung, manic, change-agent, knowledgeable.

Eight; The number of, Domineering, successful, compassionate, wise, controlling, capable, organized, ambitious, spiteful, mean, financially astute.

Nine; The number of, Intellectual, Idealist, ambitious, humanitarian, critical, perfectionist, pacifist, self absorbed, delusional, megalomaniac, extravagant, rebirth through sudden change.

Ten; The number of, a Master number and is interchangeable with the number one, but brings in the element of good fortune and increased intuitive ability, because of the addition of the zero. These individuals are; fearless, reckless, inspirational, motivational, creative, critical, and arrogant.

Eleven; The number of, a Master number.

Again, people management is a forte, and eleven is a higher vibration of the number two. These individuals are; clever, diplomatic nurturing, supportive, organized, self effacing, witty, humorous, lazy, as well as philanthropic.

Twenty-two; The number also considered to be a Master number, and a higher vibration of the number four. It contains all the elements of the four, but also includes unlimited opportunities for material success.

Pythagoras considered the number twenty-two to be the perfect number, capable of self- healing, as well as having the ability to heal others.

Thirty-three; is also a Master number and a higher vibration of the six, but, with more intense creativity, and success is experienced on the world stage, as opposed to creativity being limited to the family, and professional sphere. It is brilliance personified.

The previous two master numbers do not appear on a Numerology Chart, but are reduced to their smaller numbers, of four and six, to accommodate the limited scope of the chart.

To find your date of birth life-path number, simply add up, all the digits together and bring the total to one number. The exceptions being the master numbers, ten, eleven, twenty-two and thirty-three, which remain as they are.

Example; 18/6/1964 = 1+8+6+1+9+6+4=35 = 3+5 =8.
The Life path number is 8.

21/ 3/2006 =2+1+3+2+0+0+6 =14=1+4=5

The life path number is 5.

The changes in your numerology chart are likened to a pyramid, with each, nine year change, building on the previous one, using up the numbers of the birth date, until they are exhausted, and then repeating the numbers over again.

Also, the years of change are indicated at the top of each pyramid, and the number indicated at that point, is indicative of the type of change, that an individual can expect, for the following nine years.

To determine the type of change, the date of birth of the individual is separated onto three sections.

The day of birth/ the month of birth/ and the year of birth.

To calculate the changes, the month of birth is placed on the left hand side of the day of birth, while the year of birth is placed on the right hand side of the day of birth, so that the day of birth is in-between these two, and in that order.

Example; 18/ 6 /1964 becomes, 6/18/1964, further reduced to 6/9/2

The day and month are added together first, to determine the first change which is $6= 9+6= 15=1+5=6$.

So the first life change will be a six influence of creativity either through career or family as in having a baby.

The second life change will be determined by adding the year and month numbers together which is $9+2 =11= 1+1= 2$.

This is the number of service and putting the needs of others first. During this vibration there will be no personal opportunities available for career progress.

The third life change is arrived at by adding the first life change number, 6 to the second life change number, 2 and this gives a life change number of 8, the number of huge financial success through working hard in an organization

It means that the individual, under this financially auspicious number, will have unlimited opportunities for success, during this nine year period..

The next life path change is achieved, by adding the month number 6, with the year number 2, and once again, we arrive at another number 8, indicating that the owner of this particular birth-date will be a very wealthy individual.

To calculate when the life path changes begin, the life path number of each individual must be subtracted from 36, the age of maturity to indicate their personal life path change.

For a life path number 11, the number 11 subtracted from the age 36 leaves 25.

Therefore changes for a number 11, life path individual will begin at 25 and then every nine years after that, so the years of change will be first change at 25, 25 + 9= 34 for second change, 34+9= 43 for third change, 43+9= 52 for fourth change 52+9= 61 for fifth change and so on.

For a life path 8 individual, the number 8 subtracted from age 36, and leaves 28, and therefore, 28 is the first change, followed by 37 and then 37 +9= 46, and then 46+9=55, and then 55+9=64 and so on.

For a life path 6, the number 6 subtracted from 36 leaves 30 and so changes begin at 30 then 30+9= 39, followed by 39+9= 48, followed by 48+9= 57, followed by 57+9=66 and so on.

For the life path 10 individual the change begins at 26, the10 taken from 36 leaves 26 then 26+ 9= 35, followed 35+9= 44, followed by 44+9= 53 and so on.

For the life path 9 individual, 9 subtracted from 36=27 and so the first change will begin at 27, 27+9=36 for the second change, 36+9=45 for the third change, and 45+9=54 for the fourth change and so on.

The same type of calculation is done for each life path number, except for master numbers 33 and 22, as they are reduced to 6 and 4 respectively, for the purpose of subtraction from the age of maturity at 36, and the calculated years of change, thereafter, correspond, to those of the number 6, and the number 4.

There are usually rumblings of discontent, in a situation, two years prior to the actual change. According to Pythagoras, we move in nine year cycles. That means that we are giving birth to new opportunities, every nine years and everyone is alerted to the changes from their subconscious, whether it a feeling of discontent or in a dream.

The numerology chart itself has not been addressed here, but will be at a later date.

The following examples provide insight into the possible use of numbers by the dreaming mind.

One of my clients, asked me for advice, regarding a disturbing dream involving two black, four-wheel drive cars, which she owned in the dream, one of which, crashed against a wall.

I explained that the number two represents good, personal, or business relationships and that the number four represents, a firm foundation for success.

A car in a dream represents the dreamer herself, and the way she is moving forward in her life, at this particular moment in time.

A wall in this particular dream represents an obstacle of some kind, and the fact that one of the four-wheel drive, cars, crashed into a wall, indicates, that one of her two current business opportunities, will not be successful at this point in time.

The client's dream, was warning her, of the consequences of failing to correct her present course of action. The client was being advised that she was overstretching herself or her resources.

The interesting aspect of this dream, was the client's own life-path number, eight.

The number eight is a favourite of the Chinese, cultural, belief system, as it represents financial success.

According to Pythagoras, the number eight indicates the ability to be successful, by dominating the environment; however my client's dream, was clearly a warning about the consequences of, overstretching herself.

Unfortunately, for those whose life-path is number eight, success in the material world that is their birthright, often comes at a cost, to their personal relationships.

This is because the very thing that makes the number 8 person, successful in the material world, creates disharmony for them in their personal relationships.

The attention to detail and the abhorrence of wastefulness in any form, for the number 8 life path person, can often lead to misunderstandings and hurt feelings all round, by what may appear to be a criticism of the lifestyle of others, but which in fact, is merely an attempt to point out, unnecessary wastefulness.

An example of this was a father's concern for his thirty year-old son's, penchant, for buying new mobile phones.

When his son bought a new mobile phone, the father pointed out that the young man, already had several mobile phones, and was wasting his money, by continuing to splurge on the latest models. The son took exception to his father telling him what to do, with his money, and so refused to communicate with his father, which upset the father greatly.

When the father asked me for advice, I was able to share insight into the situation from a dream that I had, in relation to the situation.

In the dream, I had seen the father lying dead on the bed, with blood pouring from his forehead, and beside him on the bed, my son, at the age of eight asleep.

I left the room, and went to tell my mother, that the man was dead, but when she and I returned to the room, he was alive again.

Blood pouring from the head, indicates that the father thinks that the son is being emotionally abusive, by his sulky behaviour.

Changes are necessary in the way the father thinks about the situation, if he wishes, to maintain the relationship with his son. He must learn not to judge, what he considers to be his son's extravagant behaviour.

This is symbolized by the man's death, which represents the death of the relationship, as it is.

The change in how the father thinks, creating a change in the relationship with his son is represented by the father being alive once more, when my mother returns to the bedroom with me, representing unconditional mother love.

The bedroom represented the father's intimate life.

The image of my son, seen in the dream at the age of eight, represented the man, a life- path eight number, and his son, who is a life-path ten number, like my son, as well as indicating, the childishness of the situation.

When a person is asleep in a dream, it indicates that the person is unavailable in some way, which represented the estranged situation, of the son is not talking to his father.

The son, who is an Aries, astrology sign, enjoys spending his hard, earned money and resents his father, questioning his choices and life style, and so, though well intentioned, his father's interference is not welcome.

Unfortunately, the reaction of the son is a typical reaction of many family members, to those on the life-path eight and as previously mentioned, many misunderstandings, and hurt feelings often ensue, despite good intentions.

Other aspects of the number eight include compassion, wisdom, independence and self control, as well as, remarkable organizational skills.

If anyone is lucky enough to have an employee who is an eight, they can be assured that their resources are in good hands, as people born into an eight life path, will never be found guilty of waste, and can be trusted to work independently for the greater good.

By the same token, any employee, who has the life-path, number four, will be a workaholic, in any organization that they are employed in, and never leave anything half done.

Their attention to detailed work is amazing, and having unlimited amounts of energy, as their birthright, they are very busy people and as children, need to be occupied, or they might get into mischief.

The number eight, and number four, makes a formidable team, as they share similar value systems, when it comes to money, but while the number four is self-effacing and modest, the eight, likes all the trappings of success and likes to flaunt it.

The number four life-path person is a true eccentric and has the temperament and skill of an artist. They patiently work at whatever creative task gives them pleasure, and they possess the ability to shine, in an artistic and creative way.

Life-path four individuals feel situations very intensely, but are unable to verbally express their emotions, channelling them instead, into their creative projects and artistic endeavours.

Number four life-path people are also very practical people, who feel a sense of responsibility, for the happiness of others, with whom they are in a relationship and are always of service to them. Their good-natured approach to life is often taken advantage of, and so they need to exercise a sense of caution, when dealing with others.

Unfortunately, this sense of responsibility, can overwhelm number four life-path people, and can lead to feelings of depression, or negativity.

This is one of the reasons that the Chinese consider the number four to be unlucky, as it appears to be all work and no play, for this life-path number, as they are very busy people and constantly need to be doing something.

As the proverb goes

'All work and no play, makes Jack a dull boy'.

This proverb illustrates the need, for life-path four people, to relax more, and enjoy life, and share there earthy, sense of humour with others.

As both eight, and four, are life path numbers of individuals who are preoccupied, with the material side of life, they need to guard against the danger of becoming too obsessed with money, or being too greedy, and perhaps, like the lady with the two four wheel drive cars, sabotage their opportunities, by taking on too much at one time.

The number two life-path is one of service and diplomacy.

It is the life-path of individuals, who usually become part of a huge organization, which can appreciate their loyalty and diligence.

They are usually very intuitive, and like to work at their own pace, and like those on the number four life-path prefer to be self-effacing and work behind the scenes.

The intuitive number two, aspect of the dream, indicated the dreamer's own intuition, that was warning her, that she was over reaching her ability to be successful, in what she was currently engaged in.

Numbers in dreams, can also identify for us, the circumstances surrounding a particular illness, or physical ailment.

When my younger son, suffered the painful inconvenience, of an ingrown toenail, on the big toe, of his left foot, the doctor scheduled an operation for its removal, warning my son, that it was a painful procedure.

My son, who was fourteen at the time, was not looking forward to the operation, and this was causing him a great deal of concern, and he told me, that he did not want to have the operation.

I said, with the utmost conviction, "We will cure the problem now".

I went into the bathroom, where I ran a bath of warm water, into which I put, the oil of peppermint, which has antiseptic qualities, as well as the oil of rosemary, for remembrance.

As soon as my son got into the bath, his knees became cold, despite the warm water.

I told him, that as knees represented attitudes, according to Louise Hay in her book, "You Can Heal Your Life", there must be something, which he needed to change his attitude to.

After his bath, he went to bed. The next morning, he told me about a dream that he had, in which a doctor, had put ten needles into his head, and told him that he was cured.

I told my son that, as ten is the life-path number of his older brother, and as the head represents how we think about a situation; then the way he perceived his relationship with his older brother, was affecting, how he was emotionally moving forward in life, symbolized by the big toe, with its ingrown toenail.

As the big toe also provides us with balance, I told my younger son, that he had an unbalanced perspective towards the behaviour of his brother, as his expectations of him were too unrealistic.

I knew that my younger son was often disappointed, that his older brother was too busy, to spend more time with him, despite many promises to do so, and frequently let him down.

I explained to my younger son, that because his brother was three years older than him, his brother, preferred to hang out with friends of his own age, but that did not mean, that he did not care for his younger brother, it was just something that siblings often do.

I ran a warm bath for a second time and, once more put in oil of rosemary, and oil of peppermint, and then my son got back into the bath.

Remarkably, once in the bath, he was able to pull back the offending toenail, and cut out the spur.

He never did, have to have the operation, and the doctor was amazed at the change in circumstances.

The power of the mind and a change of attitude, were clearly responsible for what happened, and the ability to identify the heart of the matter, through numerology made the whole process much simpler.

I also, have no doubt that my son, like most children, who trust their mothers, believed me, when I told him, that we were going to cure the problem now, and so this trust and belief, enabled him to cure himself.

The relationship that my older son had, with his younger brother, was not unusual, as certain life-path numbers, vibrate together better than others.

My older son is a life-path ten, or one, depending on your perspective and individuals on

this particular life-path are here to enjoy life, and to help everyone to do the same.

As a consequence they are very popular individuals, and much in demand.

Their friends appear to be more important to them, than their family, as they are an extremely sociable number.

It is also the life path number of fortunate individuals, who constantly land on their feet, and no matter how grim circumstances may appear, they will always have opportunities involving love and money.

This is most likely, because they have the courage to step outside, normal conventional restrictions, and take opportunities, that others might balk at.

As a number ten, these individuals have balanced their masculine and feminine energies, symbolized by the masculine 'I' and the feminine '0'. They also possess a highly developed intuition, and sixth sense.

They have a driving need, for personal freedom and to throw off, any perceived restrictions, and so they often have problems with making commitments.

Those on the number ten life-paths are intensely creative individuals, but their need to have so much individual freedom, may prevent these individuals, from achieving the success that they are capable achieving.

In contrast, to the life-path, of his older brother, my younger son has a life path number of '9'.

It is the life-path number of people, who are the epitome of responsibility, and who will always champion the underdog. The life path number nine is honest, to the point of being naïve, expecting others to be as honest as them selves.

Nine is also the life-path number of the intellectual and according to Pythagoras, is the most powerful of all numbers, and is at the gateway to the astral plane.

Indeed, power is the driving force, behind the ruling nine life-path numbers, and using power responsibility, for the good of all, is their life mission.

As nine is also, the number of drive and ambition, those people who are fortunate enough to have more than one nine in their birth chart, will find that they are hungry for success, and will do what ever is necessary, to achieve their goals.

This life-path number, is also the number of idealism and zeal, and unfortunately, these individuals have a tendency, to get disillusioned by others, who do not live up to their idealised expectation of them.

Consequently, it is easy to understand how an unrealistic expectation, was, placed on my older son, by my younger son, resulting in injured feelings, as individuals on the number nine, life-path, tend to be very sensitive.

There is a saying, "Where your heart is, that is that is where your passion will lie."

Dreams are therefore, tailored in this direction, by the individual.

A young mother, who had a new born baby, as well as, a two year old child, asked me, to interpret the following dream for her.

She dreamed that she had tattoos across her chest.

On the left side of her chest, a green, five headed snake, and in the middle of her chest, a yellow cobra, and on the right side of her chest, a big sun/web design.

The snake and cobra were moving in her dream, and they were in battle with each other.

The tattoos indicate a tribal member of a particular family group, and because they were across her chest, they indicated an emotional attachment to the group.

The green snake, indicated jealousy by someone, "green with envy', possibly towards the newborn baby, and the yellow cobra, indicated a person of wisdom, and someone who had developed their connection to the three aspects of their person, body, mind and spirit, which was the mother, herself.

I explained the significance of the colour yellow, indicating a healing for someone, regarding how they were thinking about a situation, and the number five, which represented a change in a situation, as a consequence of knowledge acquired.

The web indicates the web of life, and the sun is a play on words, and refers to her two year old son, who is obviously and quite naturally so, having trouble coming to terms with his new baby sister.

The number five in the dream, was significant, as it indicated that the change needed, in the young boy's attitude, towards his sister would happen.

The number five in numerology is the number of emotional balance and strength of character, as well as personal freedom.

People, who have a life-path of five, always appear unruffled by their surroundings and never allow their emotions to get out of control, as they tend to intellectualize a situation.

As a consequence, they never sabotage their opportunities by indulging in an emotional outburst.

A dream that I had, around a situation at my place of work, illustrates this self control through knowledge, which can prevent a situation, from getting from out of hand, or being manipulated by unscrupulous individuals.

In my dream, I needed to go to the bathroom.

I seemed to be in a hospital, and as I walked through the hospital looking for a female toilet, I could only find male toilets, so I went outside the hospital, to see if I could find a female toilet somewhere in the grounds, of the hospital.

I discovered toilet-cubicles out side, that you had to climb into and after you did so, you had to put five cents into a slot and it gave you a ride.

At first I was nervous about being closed in there, as was the little girl in the cubicle next to me. I gave her the five cents necessary for the ride, but she decided against having the ride.

A man and his partner were in their car outside the ride watching, and then they left.

A different man asked me what the ride was like.

I said, "it is very tame really, but if you were with a group of people, like a group of girls, you could ham it up and make it seem more exciting than it actually was."

And then I left.

This dream referred to a difficult emotional situation at work, which needed to be addressed.

The hospital represented a place of healing, or in this case an opportunity to resolve the difficulties, in the situation.

When one is going to the toilet to urinate, the action represents being in emotional control of a situation and dealing with it in an appropriate way, and defecating can represent an opportunity, to get rid of unhealthy issues, 'letting them go' so to speak.

The five cents in the dream refers to the expression "putting your five cents worth in", in other words, contributing to a conversation by stating your personal opinion.

The ride in the dream refers to the emotional ups and downs, generated by the feelings involved, in this particular situation.

The couple in the car suggests that someone was observing the reaction of others, to the situation, or what was being said.

The car leaving, suggests that whoever was watching, did not get, or see the reaction that they expected to see.

This is validated by a further party, wanting to know what the ride was like, and the response that it was tame, but could have been hammed up by excitable females. This indicates that the emotional situation could have been blown out of all proportion, if it had not been dealt with, using the five number, of knowledge and emotional control.

As five also represents the five senses of human nature, people under a five ruling number feel the need to travel and experience life.

Acquiring knowledge is a motivational force, that drives ruling five people, and in whatever occupation they choose, they will excel, because of the breadth of knowledge and perfectionism that they bring, to their career.

It is interesting to note, that if the number five should fall in one of the peak changes of your birth chart, you will definitely feel the need to move house, at that time.

The symbolism of the snake in the dream also deserves attention, and symbolizes letting go of the past and moving on, or reinventing oneself.

I had initially thought that the son may have been born in the Chinese year of the Snake, but the young mother, said that he was born in the year of the Dragon, and the mother then said, she was not sure if it was a snake, or dragon in the dream.

I said that the Chinese often call the snake, the little dragon, but all other indicators in the dream pointed to her son's need, to adjust to the changing family circumstances, due to the arrival of the new baby.

I was impressed when I visited the grave of distant relatives in Bungonia, outside Gouldburn in New South Wales, Australia, to discover a snakeskin at the foot of the grave and which I now keep in a little jar, as a reminder of the transmigration of the soul. It was also a reminder to let go of the past and move on with life.

Indeed after my divorce, I had a dream in which I was told; that I now needed to mourn all the dead children, and I was told that there were three cupfuls of them.

The dream referred to all the childhood memories associated with my three sisters, who were represented by the feminine symbolism of the cup, and who had reacted in a negative way, towards my divorce and now I needed to come to terms with the fact, that our relationship was finished.

Often, others feel threatened when we change, as it forces them to reassess the values of their own lives and this may be too great a challenge to face, and so it is easier to avoid the person, who makes them feel uncomfortable.

One of the consequences of a divorce involves the restructuring of your whole life, as relationships built up around a particular way of life tend to disintegrate, when the dynamics of that particular life style, change.

This dream forced me to recognize, that my relationship with my sisters would never be the same again.

The number six in a dream is a significant number in relation to family members and relationships in general, as it represents the "mother" energy of creativity that is, the abundant creativity of mother earth, as well as the creativity of the individuals of the number six life-path.

I had the following dream for a young couple, who had concerns regarding their commitment, and if they were meant to stay together.

I saw an airplane with, '6 hour flight' written on it.

Some one in the dream said that, "planes don't fly so high any more, so that if they crash, people do not get so badly hurt.".

I was also told that there was only one flight a day.

Then I could see a young couple sitting together on a single bed kissing, with one in the bed, and the other sitting on top of the blankets.

This dream indicated that because of disappointments in the past, to do with this relationship, an agreement had now been reached regarding the path that their relationship would follow at the moment, due to a situation of ill health, for one of them.

The kiss indicated their feelings for each other, but the single bed indicated a failure to make the commitment to a permanent relationship.

The number six on the plane, is in fact the life path number of the young man, who had been hurt in the past and who, is now unable to commit fully, because of trust issues

The one flight a day suggests that the support is limited to the situation at hand.

Issues of trust are going to have to be worked on, if the relationship is to continue, once full health has been regained by the person who has been ill.

The person, who has a life path number of six, makes an ideal relationship partner and a doting parent.

People who have the life path, of number six, are very loyal to their families and have a need, to feel needed.

They are usually very charming individuals, and do not feel the need to make themselves look, or feel good, at another's expense and so, are popular amongst their peers, as well as family members.

They are extremely creative individuals, and when the number six appears on the birth chart, of an individual's change Peak, it indicates a career change that may, or may not, also involve a relationship, and a baby.

As creativity is the main thrust of this number, creativity in the home, or creativity in career, is the outcome, of the number six vibration.

Unfortunately those under the number six vibration, often fail to reach the heights in their creative endeavours. They have a tendency to be too concerned about the opinions of others, and to worry too much about the possibility of failure.

I often remind these people of the favourite expression of my mother and also I am sure, the favourite expression of many other mothers which is;

'What will the neighbours say?' and, as an antidote to this self sabotaging mantra, I give them my favourite piece of advice of,

'If they are not paying your bills, why would you care what they think?

The following dream illustrates the fear and anxiety, that can incapacitate the number six life-path individual and that can prevent them from achieving success in their lives.

A friend of mine, an exceptionally, well qualified schoolteacher, who had buried their talents in a junior school, was 'Head Hunted' by a much larger, more academically successful school, which could provide more career-path opportunities, in the future.

The teacher told me of their reluctance to accept the career opportunity, and I advised them to ask, to be told in their dreams, if it was in their best interests to accept the position, knowing that life-path six individuals, tend to shy away from the limelight, and prefer to work in the background.

The following dream indicated that the person would be happier, if they remained in their current position.

The person dreamed that they were in their present school, and that they were flying around the playground, with a year ten student on their back, enjoying themselves.

Suddenly the bell rang, and the teacher found themselves in the corridor, of the other school, and was having trouble locating their classroom. Their clothes were too tight, and they had trouble breathing.

Suddenly, a classroom door opened, and the teacher blurted out, "I don't want the job."

The dream scenario demonstrated that the teacher enjoyed her current position, and found pleasure in teaching a subject that she enjoyed, and where she was able to give all the support needed.

The number ten indicating how well balanced she was, and in control in her current position.

This of course, is in complete contrast to the experience in the second school, where stress and anxiety were taking control of the dreamer. The expectations of the new school, indicated by the dreamer's tight clothing, would be overwhelming for the dreamer.

The teacher concerned, had not been interested in changing schools, but I had simply suggested using the dream technique to enable the person to clarify in their own mind, the reason for the reluctance to move.

The intense anxiety of a number six life-path person can also manifest in psychosomatic illness.

One young lady that I used to know was so distraught by the collapse of her personal relationship, before her final exams at University, that she suffered temporary paralysis of her right arm, and so was unable to sit her final exams, and had to return the following year, to complete her University degree.

One of the more interesting aspects of the number six vibration however, is its magnetic attraction of luck and love.

Those individuals, who are fortunate enough, to be born under this vibration, will always, like the number ten life-path, have an abundance of love and money.

Often those of the life path number six, find happiness in relationships with individuals on the life path of the number three, whose communication skills and extravert nature are in contrast to their own.

Another aspect of numbers in the dream landscape is the indication of time.

The number may refer to a day of the week, or the amount of days, or months before an event happens, or it may also indicate a particular time of day.

It is only, by relating the dream to what is happening around the dreamer, at the time of the dream, that a correct interpretation can be made.

CHAPTER ELEVEN

Colour in Dreams

Colour plays an important part in the dream landscape.

Feelings and emotions, as well as the predisposition of a person, are often indicated by certain colours in dreams.

The following is a brief explanation of colour.

Blue
The colour blue may indicate feeling blue, if it is a bluish blue. Light blue indicates a healing and deep blue indicates a spiritually minded person.

Pink
The colour pink indicates unconditional love.

Red
Red is passion, as well as having personal power.
Fire engine red can suggest anger.

Turquoise
Turquoise represents personal freedom.

Yellow
Yellow is the colour of the intellect, as well as happiness and well-being. It is also the colour of financial success.

Green
Green can mean green with envy, emotional balance, harmony, abundance.

Magenta
Magenta is often associated psychic ability, as well as selflessness and perfection.

Orange
Orange is the colour of independence and being sociable.

Violet
Violet indicates spiritual protection, as well as nobility and respect.

White
White can indicate purity of heart, as well as sadness, and sometimes an illness, can be indicated by this colour.

Black
Black is the colour of judgment, manifestation and negativity, it indicates the material world.

Brown
Brown represents commitment and the earth and in some cases a death.

Grey
Grey is the colour of service and self effacement.

CHAPTER TWELVE

Astrological Characteristics

Aries the Ram. March 21-April 20
Generous, honest, justice oriented, childlike, talkative, spontaneous,
Negative traits; lack of staying power, spendthrift, impatience,
indiscreet, quick tempered, impulsive.

Taurus the Bull. April 21-May 21
Dependable, hardworking, good-natured, patient, artistic, domestic.
Negative traits; possessive, stubborn, self-indulgent, inflexible,
greedy.

Gemini the Twins. May 22-June 22
Clever, enterprising, witty, sociable, busy, logical.
Negative traits; unpunctual, unreliable, gossiping, restless, tense
nervous.

Cancer the Crab. June 23-July 23
Home-loving, nurturing, ambitious, sensitive, charitable,
protective, tenacious.
Negative traits; clingy, jealous, manipulative, fussy, indirect moody.

Leo the Lion. July 24– August 23
Courageous, strong-willed, natural leader, generous, daring, popular.
Negative traits; pompous, spendthrift, self-centred, bossy, patronizing.

Virgo the Virgin. August 24– September 23
Precise, devoted, meticulous, hardworking, loving, fanatically tidy.
Negative traits; cold, critical, reserved, fearful, judgmental, jealous.

Libra the Scales. September 24–October 23
Balanced, perceptive, logical, respectful, civilized, charming.
Negative traits; opinionated, gullible, mercenary, promiscuous, lacking conviction, superficial.

Scorpio the Scorpion. October 24– November 22
Generous, dramatic, intuitive, loyal, stubborn, thoughtful.
Negative traits; jealousy, suspicious, secretive, self-pitying, angry, possessive.

Sagittarius the Centaur. November 23– December 21
Lucky, impulsive, independent, outgoing, broad-minded, straightforward.
Negative traits; impatient, aggressive, irrational, selfish, impetuous.

Capricorn the Goat. December 22– January 20
Ambitious, dedicated, honest, focused, disciplined, logical, hard- working.
Negative traits; controlling, calculating, pessimistic, miserly, retaliatory.

Aquarius the Water Bearer. January 21– February 19
Brilliant, friendly, open-minded, spontaneous, tolerant, whimsical.

Negative traits; lacking commitment, cold, aloof, mean spirited, fickle, self-centered.

Pisces the Fish February 20- March 20
Altruistic, sensitive, intuitive, creative, lucky, spiritual.
Negative traits; weak-willed, vague, depressed, needy, manipulative, duplicitous.

CHAPTER THIRTEEN

General Symbols found in Dreams

House

The house in a dream represents the dreamer, so the type of house is very important as it relates to the spiritual life and aspirations of the dreamer.

The sitting-room represents the social life, the kitchen the nurturing aspects, the hallway meeting people, the bathroom represents cleansing, the toilet emotional control and letting go of issues, and the bedroom, the intimate life of the dreamer.

The attic represents memories, the ceiling can represent how we think, as can the roof which gives protection to the way we think, and the basement can represent our subconscious, while the garage represents the skills and talents that we have.

The stairway of a house represents the progress that we are making in any area of our lives, climbing is moving forward, while descending can represent either descending into our subconscious, or encountering difficulties with what we are doing.

Doors and windows may represent opportunities, or a different perspective on a situation.

Furniture in a house represents our value system, and what is important to us.

Body

The body is a good indicator of our spiritual progress and is an easy yard stick to use.

Any problem in a dream or even in our conscious life, with the body, could indicate a problem in a particular aspect of our lives.

The head is how we think, the eyes are how we see, the ears how we listen, the nose our intuition, mouth our nurturing ability, the face is how we present ourselves to the world.

The neck joins the head to the body and indicates how we think and feel about a situation.

It is by combining the head with the heart that we have true wisdom.

Anything that we wear around our neck in a dream indicates that others are affecting the way that we think, and feel about a situation.

An example of this is a dream I had alerting me to the need to nurture my younger son more after my divorce, as he was having great difficulty adjusting to the change in the family circumstances.

Parts of the Body

The limbs of the body indicate gender issues and the torso or trunk of the body, the support system.

The breasts are also a nurturing aspect of the female body, as are the hips.

The hands represent how we take hold of life and each finger of the hand represents an aspect of our personality.

The thumb is your personal power, the index finger the ego and career success, the middle finger justice issues, and the ring finger, relationships, while the little finger communication, and the palm of the hand temperament and success.

The feet represent, how well grounded we are, and the toes of the feet, correspond to the fingers of the hand.

Clothes

Clothes that we wear, also represent our value system and how well protected, we are.

Shoes also represent being grounded as well as status, and colour is significant in both cases.

Emotions

Emotions in dreams can be indicated by water, and so careful attention should be paid to how calm, shallow, stormy or deep the water is.

Flying

Flying dreams often indicate that the dreamer is accessing their personal power, and feeling in control of their lives.

When there is any discomfort in the dream or problem, the dreamer's self confidence may be in question, or his capacity to deal with a situation.

Blood

Blood in dreams often indicates some type of abuse such as emotional or psychological, unless it has to do with female menstruation, which is a natural cycle of female life.

Dream context and circumstances of the dreamer need to be carefully considered here.

Pregnancy

Pregnancy also needs careful consideration in the context of the dreamer's conscious life.

Is the dreamer in a position to get pregnant, or is the pregnancy telling the dreamer that new opportunities are stirring in the waters of creativity, for advancement in the dreamer's professional life?

In the latter context, men as well as women can dream of being pregnant.

Animal dreams

Animals in dreams may be alerting us to people, who are behaving in such a way, that they are displaying the traits of particular animals, or perhaps we need to utilize these traits ourselves.

It is also important to note whether the animal in our dream is wild or domesticated, the age of the animal and whether young or old and our feelings towards the animal in our dream.

Also the association of animals sacred to special deities needs to be considered.

The following is the context in which animals may appear, depending on the circumstances in the dreamer's life, at the time of the dream.

Rat; disloyal behavior, acquisitive, social.
Ox; long suffering, hard working, patient.

Tiger; intuitive, predator, good sense of self, royality.
Rabbit; intuitive, fertility, children, timid good natured.
Dragon; mother issues.
Snake; rebirth, sexuality, deceit, enemy.

Horse; persistence, harnessing personal power.
Goat; sexuality, creativity, ambition, acting the goat.
Monkey; clever, deceitful, playful, cheeky.
Rooster; arrogance, pride, inflated sense of self.
Dog; loyalty, guardian of the under world, or uncontrolled instincts.
Pig; bringing home the bacon as in career success, or self indulgence.
Cat; intuition, gossip, rival.
Leopard; cruelty and aggression.
Lizard; cold blooded.
Frog; a period of change.
Sheep; following others, gentle.
Lion; courage as in lion hearted.
Bull; stubborn, territorial.

Insects

Insects seen in a dream frequently alerts the dreamer to negative thoughts or feelings that they are holding towards a particular situation.
Insects, can also represent unhealthy situations.

Money

Finding money in dreams indicates growth in self esteem.

Teeth
Loss of teeth can represent a fear of growing old, or problems, with the dreamer's self image.
The back teeth often refer to family issues.

Sex

Sexual encounters in a dream often refer to some aspect of the personality that needs to be integrated.

Sex in a dream rarely means the sexual act, but is usually referring to a situation where the dreamer is getting closer emotionally, to a partner.

Dancing with a partner also has a similar meaning, as dancing refers to being in touch with the natural rhythm of life.

Singing

Singing in a dream represents being in touch with the feeling side of life and being able to express ourselves.

Muscles

Building muscles in a dream refers to developing emotional muscles or strength.

Wedding

Getting married in a dream often refers to the mystic marriage of the union between the female and male aspects of one's nature, and becoming a whole person.

Puns

Often the dream image will involve a play on words and the dreamer needs to be aware of this.

The following examples should help the dreamer.

Floor/flaw, rites/rights, mail/male, sun/son, sun burnt/ negatively affected by the son, while to be putting on make-up or taking it off, maybe a play on words regarding a reconciliation after an argument, or a falling out, in a relationship.

Ultimately, the dreamer him/herself will have a better understanding of the symbolism in a dream as it relates to them, and their personal experiences, and what is happening around them in their external life, at the time of the dream.

The message that the dream is trying to convey needs to be analyzed.

Is it simply giving insight into the happenings of the previous day, that the conscious mind was unaware of, or is the dream trying to convey a much deeper meaning about the dreamer's lifestyle and opportunities for success?

The diet of the dreamer may also need to be considered when analyzing a dream, as certain foods or substances taken in the evening may be impacting on the dreamer.

Even a simple thing like room temperature, can affect the dream content, so check everything out, presume nothing and trust only a well developed higher self.

RECOMMENDED READING

Allen, Stephen, Lords of Battle Osprey Publishing 2007

Ball, Pamela, 10,000 Dreams Interpreted Arcturus Publishing Limited 1996

Brewer's Dictionary of Phrase & Fable Cassell LTD. London 1972

Butler, W. E. Magic It's Ritual, Power and Purpose The Aquarian Press, Wellingborough, Northamptonshire 1977

Bly, Robert, Iron John Element Rockport Massachusetts 1990

Castaneda, Carlos, The Teachings Of Don Juan Penguin Books 1970

The Art Of Dreaming Harper Collins 1993

Cavendish, Richard, Man Myth & Magic BPC Publishing Ltd.

The Tarot Chancellor Press 1986

Cayce, Edgar, The Edgar Cayce Collection Random House 1968

Handbook for Health Through Drugless Therapy Mac Millan Publishing Company 1971

Cheiro's Language of The Hand Prentice Hall Press 1987

Cleary, Thomas, The Art Of War Shambhala Dragon Editions 1988

Cotterell, Arthur, The Encyclopedia Of Mythology Hermes House 2001

Cunningham' Encyclopedia Of Magical Herbs Llewellyn Worldwide Publications 2002

Davies, Rodney, Fortune Telling By Palmistry Harper Collins Publishers 1987

Delaney, Frank, Legends Of The Celts Grafton, Harper Collins 194

Estes, Clarissa Pinkola, Women Who Run With Wolves Rider 1992

Fontana, David, The Secret Language Of Dreams Duncan Baird Publishers 1994
Frankl, Viktor E. 1946 Man's Search for Meaning

Goodman, Linda, Linda Goodman's Signs Pan Books 1972

Halevi, Z'ev ben Shimon, Tree Of Life Gateway Books 1997

Hay, L. Hay, You Can Heal your Life Specialist Publications Australia 1988

Hemmes, Hilda, Herbs with Hilde Hemmes South Australian School of Herbal Medicine 1992

Holy Bible Cambridge:Printed At The University Press

Hyde Maggie and Mc Guinness, Michael, Introducing Jung Totem Books USA 1997

Jung, Carl G. Man and his Symbols Aldus Books 1964
Memories, Dreams, Reflections London U.K. New York Routledge (Fontana Paperback Edition 1967).

Laidler, Keith, The Head Of God Weidenfeld & Nicolson 1998
Leonard, Linda Schierse The Wounded Woman Shambhala Publications Inc. Boston & London 1998

McKenna, Breige, Healing Faith Transforms Our Fears
Massey, Gerald Ancient Egypt the Light of the World.

Phillip, David A. Dr. Secrets of The Inner Self Angus & Robertson Publishers 1980

Peale, Norman Vincent, The Power of Positive Thinking The Chaucer Press 1968

Phillip, Neil, Myths & Fairy Tales Collection Dorling Kindersley 1999

Riso, Don Richard, Discovering Your Personality Type Houghton Mifflin Company 1995

Scheimann Eugene MD & Altman Nathaniel, Medical Palmistry The Aquarian Press
1989

Scully, Nicki The Golden Cauldron Bear & Company, Inc. Santa Fe, 1991

Shine, Betty, Mind Magic Corgi Books 1993

Shinn, Florence Scovel, Wisdom of Florence Scovel Shinn Simon& Schuster 1989

Somerville, Neil, Your Chinese Horoscope 2000 Harper Collins Publisher1999

Vollmar, Klaus, The Little Giant Encyclopedia Of Dream Symbols Stirling Publishing Co., Inc. 1997

Walker, Barbara G. The Woman's Dictionary of Symbols and Sacred Objects Pandora Harper Collins Publisher 1988

Webster, Richard, Past- Life Memories Llewellyn Publications 2001

Zolar's House Of The Spirits Prentice Hall 1987

EPILOGUE

From the information that I have received in my dreams, I believe that we move through life in Soul groups, and that each member of that Soul group, has the ability to move the whole group forward, each time that individual Soul, follows the messages given to them in their dreams that require courage in the face of adversity.

The truth of this was made known to me in my dreams around the time of my divorce.

Prior to getting a divorce, I had a very vivid dream in which it was night time, and I was flying through the air and I seemed to be blind.

Some one in the dream said to me "Open your eyes and look at the journey."

To which I replied, "I don't need to, God has me by the heels."

Then I was set down outside a castle, and I could hear loud cheering coming from within.

In the dream I realized that it was because of me, that everyone was cheering and that it was because of me, that they had managed to get here.

My Irish Catholic upbringing had created a huge hurdle for me to overcome, as divorce was an unthinkable course of action and women were expected to remain stoically in their marriage, despite untenable situations.

I myself had thought "I will have to die to get out of this marriage, because I am a Catholic from Northern Ireland.

Then I had a dream telling me that I would die, if I didn't get out of the marriage and that changed everything.

Women often stay in unhappy marriages and become ill, rather than face the consequences of getting a divorce.

My dream assured me that in the long run everyone would benefit from my courage to change the 'status quo.'

By having the courage to get a divorce,

I changed the dynamics in my family's attitude to relationships and the outworn belief system, which forced women to stay in unhappy marriages, regardless of the personal cost, and so despite condemnation from family and friends, I knew in my heart that I had done the right thing.

May God hold you close in the palm of his hand!

ABOUT THE AUTHOR

With a Masters of Applied Science, a Post Graduate Degree and a Teacher's Certificate in Education, Rosemary Dawson is a Dream Catcher' par excellence'.

A high-school teacher with over thirty years of experience and a thriving motivational, meditation and psychic development business in Sydney, Australia, Rosemary, by using an incredibly simple technique to access information in her dreams, has combined the messages that she received in her dreams with orthodox medicine, to overcome the potentially crippling condition of rheumatoid arthritis and scleroderma.

Rosemary now shares this simple technique with you in her book, Rosin Dubh, The Irish Dream Catcher.

Printed in the United States
By Bookmasters